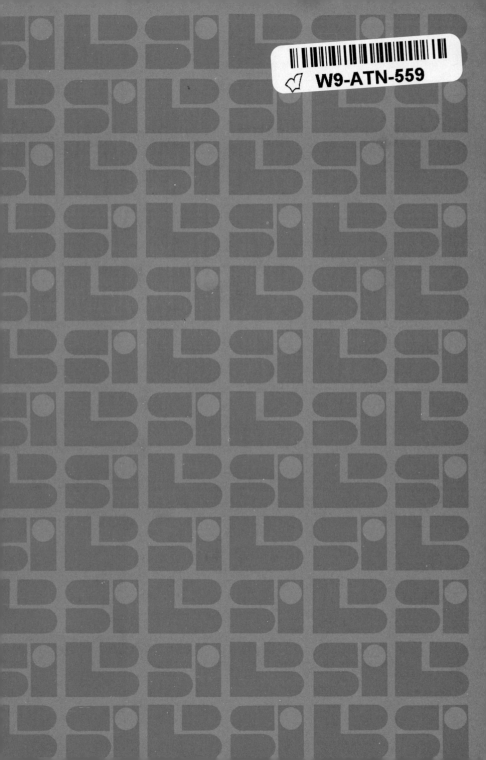

## Books by Dan Jenkins

*The Best 18 Golf Holes in America*

*The Dogged Victims of Inexorable Fate*

*Saturday's America*

# Saturday's
# America

# DAN JENKINS

## Saturday's America

*A Sports Illustrated Book*

BOSTON • LITTLE, BROWN AND COMPANY • TORONTO

LIBRARY OF CONGRESS CATALOG CARD NO. 78–121437

01374 WO 461 T 10/70

*Third Printing*

Sports Illustrated Books
are published by
Little, Brown and Company
in association with
Sports Illustrated Magazine

*Published simultaneously in Canada
by Little, Brown & Company (Canada) Limited*

PRINTED IN THE UNITED STATES OF AMERICA

*This book probably should be dedicated
to a lot of old friends in the publicity
business, like JONES RAMSEY and JIM BROCK,
who have made my work so easy and
pleasant over the years, or to coaches
like DARRELL ROYAL and ABE MARTIN, who
have done the same thing. But surely
they won't begrudge me the opportunity
of dedicating it to three little bench-
warmers named SALLY, MARTY and DANNY —
in the hope that they learn to relish
each autumn Saturday as I have.*

When the one great scorer comes to write against your name, it matters a whole hell of a lot whether you win or lose.

A LOT OF COACHES

When you're playing for the national championship, it's not a matter of life or death. It's more important than that.

DUFFY DAUGHERTY

A coach likes to have a lot of those old trained pigs who'll grin and jump right in the slop for him.

DARRELL ROYAL

When we have a good team at Alabama, I know it's because we have boys who come from good Mamas and Papas.

BEAR BRYANT

I've checked my heart. I don't have one.

JOHN MCKAY

I've never known of a football writer who ever had to stand up to a blitz.

JOE NAMATH

# Acknowledgment

All of the material in this book is either based upon stories, or consists of parts of stories, which were carried up and down the halls of *Sports Illustrated* a number of times and then published. The men who most often carried the stories, and frequently made them clearer, were Andrew Crichton, Ray Cave and Walter Bingham, who happen to be editors for whom I have a high regard. They are listed in the order that I first caught them lifting what they said were excessive insults out of my copy. The final approval for the publication of the material in both magazine and hard-cover form, however, was granted by Andre Laguerre, our managing editor. If football is any better off because of his judgment, I am pleased. But the sport could never be as indebted to Andre as I am.

*D. J.*

# Contents

# Saturday's America

# 1

## Saturday's America

*Ecstatic moments in the life of a football writer who alienated whole communities.*

**O**N the wall of a twentieth-floor office in one of those thrilling Manhattan skyscrapers — the kind King Kong liked to cling to — there is a fan letter elegantly framed and prominently displayed. It hangs there to remind anyone writing about the passionate game of college football that the rewards of the job are ecstatic. The letter says:

*Mr. Dan Jenkins*
*c/o Sports Illustrated*
*Time & Life Building*
*Rockefeller Center*
*New York, New York*

*Dear Sir:*
  *Notre Dame 51, Southern California 0.*
  *Go straight to HELL! You lousy son of a bitch!*

It happens to be my very favorite letter of all time, and I find myself constantly drawing on it for inspiration. However, there are interludes when it doesn't furnish me exactly what I need. Thus, I turn toward another wall in the room and gaze at the glossy print of an old UPI photograph which shows in all of its fun-loving splendor a group of Notre Dame students burning twelve hundred copies of *Sports Illustrated* that contained, one certain week, another of my essays on the Fighting Irish.

Since I am frequently given to daydreaming, these treasures often stir my memories. And now, in this moment, I find myself backpedaling to other Saturdays. I am writing again bits and chunks of literature which have alienated whole communities . . .

SOUTH BEND, Indiana

Maybe the Vatican ought to consider banning Purdue instead of The Pill. Maybe Purdue is the hugest, fleetest, calmest and most skilled football team that ever tromped through the Indiana sycamores. Maybe Leroy Keyes is the greatest quadruple threat since Mount Rushmore. And maybe Notre Dame would be better off trying to win one for Ara Parseghian instead of the Gipper.

The whole scene was set up perfectly for Notre

Dame. The Irish were at home, all nestled comfortably in that cavern of devotion known as the Notre Dame Stadium, and they had a running game they had lacked. The weather was clear and sport-jacket comfortable and Pat O'Brien had spoken at the Friday night pep rally and done his Gipper thing, and Notre Dame wanted these Purdue people badly because of last year's loss. There were even these signs and banners strewn around the campus commanding Parseghian's legions to do some very un-Catholic things to Purdue — and the Golden Girl, too.

But there was only one thing wrong with all this. Purdue wades into all of this South Bend lore like it goes to the drugstore. A Purdue man comes from only two hours down the road. He has heard the "Victory March" so often he thinks it's a deodorant commercial. He is big, brooding, nonchalant, confident, and he has people like Leroy Keyes and Mike Phipps going for him, and what he does is, he turns a big game against what is supposed to be the No. 1 team into a barn dance.

FAYETTEVILLE, Arkansas

Aw, yew bet. They got White River channel cat that Frank Broyles likes better than steak, and strawberries as big and red as the nose on a Saturday night beer drinker in Possum Grape. They got fried chicken so tender and flavory it makes a man want to weep. There's good duck hunting and better fishing. You mean you ain't never throwed a hook in Bull Shoals? There's the Watermelon Festival in Hope, the Grape Festival in Tontitown, the Diamond Cave in Jasper, the Bracken Ridge Lodge Doll Museum in Eureka Springs and the Oil Jubilee in Magnolia. Didn't General Douglas MacArthur get hisself born in Little Rock? And wasn't there Fay Templeton, the actress, and Bob Burns, the comedian, and Albert Pike, the writer? It wasn't as though the state never had anything to be proud of before Frank Broyles taught the Razorbacks to bristle and snout. But God love Frank Broyles and don't cash his personal check. Frame it. He done beat Texas in the big one.

## COLUMBIA, Missouri

Missouri's Dan Devine looked like a man who had just learned that his disease was incurable. He was leaning against a table in the silent gloom of his locker room, a towel around his neck, a paper cup of water in his hand, whip-dog tired, and his large brown eyes fixed vacantly on a lot of things that could have happened. He talked softly and very, very slowly. "I don't think . . . I can remember . . . a team of ours ever playing this well . . . and

losing," he said. "But, well, they . . . they just . . .
they somehow do a number of things real well."
*They* were the ponderous, relentless, ill-attired Corn-
huskers of Nebraska, and this is how they left you
after a football game.

Devine had got them in his own stadium on a
warm, picturesque homecoming day before the
largest crowd, 58,000, ever to see a sports event in
his state. It was the perfect upset situation. He had
also got them 14–0 down in the first quarter with a
poised, vicious, thoroughly dedicated team of his
own that featured the talents of Gary Lane and
Johnny Roland. But he had somehow lost, 16–14, in
the last five minutes, and the only explanation
seemed to be that Nebraska was overwhelming.
Clumsy but overwhelming.

Indeed, this was the kind of team Bob Devaney
had put together out in Lincoln: big, mobile, deep,
patient, mysteriously unemotional, workmanlike and
confident. Nebraska was so big that when the Corn-
huskers ran out there, you could see the field tilt.
Their uniforms were ugly with skinny numerals and
their socks slipped down, and they stood around a lot
at times, but there were moments when the ball was
snapped that wild, wonderful things happened. They
were headed for a 10–0 season, and when a young

man named Larry Wachholtz place-kicked the winning field goal, a couple of Nebraska players were
actually seen jumping up and down on the sideline.

Upstairs, Don Bryant, the Nebraska publicity
man, was startled. "Look," he said. "They almost look
like students."

SOUTH BEND, Indiana

The day of the Poll Bowl was sunny and pleasant,
as Knute or Grantland would have ordered it, and
into this tunnel of love that is sometimes called
Notre Dame Stadium came this monstrous Fighting
Irish football team in the blue shirts and gold hats —
a team that had been picked by everyone from the
sausage stringers of Padua to the cleaning ladies of
Bunkie, Louisiana, as the best in the whole world.
The opponent was a familiar old enemy named
Southern California, which, incidentally, had a
better team because of a guy named O. J. Simpson,
but there is no logic in South Bend on fall Saturdays.
When Notre Dame has decent material and is playing at home amid all of that love, and spirit, and
ghosts, and mystery, it must win. Especially if it has
athletes. And it *did* have some athletes, didn't it?

Apparently not. In the biggest game of the year
before a full house of 59,000 worshippers, Notre
Dame turned up without a runner, without a passer

and without a kicker, three things that a football team sort of, well, needs. Finally, then, when O.J. had finished doing his thing, and the Fighting Irish were thoroughly beaten, there was at least one man in town who could be philosophical. Roger Valdiserri, the Notre Dame publicity man, managed to smile painfully.

"They say his nickname is Orange Juice," Roger said of Simpson. "But the O. J. ought to stand for Oh, Jesus, as in 'Oh, Jesus, there he goes again.' "

KNOXVILLE, Tennessee

The question of whether a good football game can be played on your living room carpet has been answered pretty much to everyone's satisfaction down on a rim of the Smokies in the Old South. The University of Tennessee has won the sport's interior decorating award with its new synthetic turf, and it has also managed to tie a game against Georgia with no time left on the clock. There at the end of it all with this fellow named Bubba Wyche, the Tennessee quarterback, throwing a touchdown pass and then a two-point conversion pass for the 17–17 deadlock, everything sagged mercifully except the gleaming nylon playing field. It was still as rich green and spotless as it had been three hours earlier. And this was after a truckload of Tennessee cheerleaders had driven on it, after a Tennessee walking horse had pranced around it, after a Georgia bulldog had gnawed at it, and after a Georgia coach had flicked ashes on it. It was even after a Negro had played on it, which hadn't happened every day in the Southeastern Conference. So the verdict had to be that artificial turf was glorious. God blew it when he gave us grass.

UNIVERSITY PARK, Pennsylvania

A Beethoven symphony swirls through the head of a defensive tackle. A linebacker earnestly dashes off to physics class on the morning of a game. Test tubes intrigue a cornerback. Math fascinates a center. Engineering problems make a halfback swoon. And while the youthful keeper of all these characters, Penn State's Joe Paterno, should be fretting about his team's ascent in the ratings or a bowl bid, he stared at the boutique-colored leaves of the pastoral Alleghenies, thought about the romantic poets, and longed to drive his kids over to Waddle or Martha Furnace so they could sit down and talk to a cow. Was it possible that this atmosphere could have produced the best team the East had seen in years? You could bust everybody in Potters Mills if it wasn't.

Joe Paterno was not a coach who put his soul in a pickle jar if something bad happened. He liked for his teams to have fun and do crazy things, like gamble on fourth down and go for two-point conversions when they shouldn't. He liked for them to slop around like this, barely beating a mediocre Army team 28–24, and have one of them tell him, "You know what, Coach? You almost blew it."

All Penn State did was win. And all Paterno did was have fun and see to it that his players had fun. "All I tell them about getting up for a game is that this is the only time in their lives when 50,000 people are going to cheer them for doing something," he said. "So far as winning honors for me, that's baloney."

Paterno came from Brooklyn and he looked and talked like a detective, but what he said kept making sense. "You know what happens when you're Number One? Nobody is happy until you're Number One *again,* and that might be never. Coach of the Year? That would mean I'd make some money and I'd have a fourteen thousand dollar mortgage instead of an eighteen thousand dollar mortgage. Big deal."

What about the winning streak?

"Look outside," Paterno said. "The leaves are turning."

BLOOMINGTON, Indiana

All around Indiana everybody said to keep the big red ball rolling, and handed you a little red ball. Everybody was afraid to change clothes and was looking for lucky pennies. Everybody was making reservations for Pasadena and the Rose Bowl. Everybody was praying their punter would — please — punt. Everybody was doing all this because a football phenomenon had overflowed the banks of the Wabash and although there were a few undemented people who felt that reality was about to set in, it might not. For as everybody in Indiana said, God was alive and playing defensive end for the Hoosiers.

What had happened was that Indiana University, a school with about as much romance in its football history as a stone quarry, had won seven games in a row after it sneaked by Wisconsin 14–9, and Indiana did not usually win seven games in seven years. In fact, Indiana's record in football ranked right up there with Germany's record in world wars. Its history was so depressing that its fans had learned to look back with fondness on the glory-filled year of 1958 when Indiana managed a 5–3–1 record. But there were the Hoosiers now, 7–0, right up there in the ratings, and probably headed for Pasadena with a loony gang of sophomores who disobeyed their coach, Johnny Pont, at practically every turn, and who somehow won every game in the last crazy, bewildering moment.

"All I know is, we're uninhibited and unexpected," said Pont. "I ask my players what they're going to do to us next, and they just giggle. I'm sure they don't know."

What Indiana probably needed was Alfred Hitchcock for a coach. It had beaten Kentucky 12–10 when a fourth-down pass had been deflected — yes — into a receiver's hands for a touchdown. It had beaten Kansas 18–15 on a field goal by a substitute kicker because the regular had come up with an arthritic toe. It had beaten Illinois 20–7 on a fumble. It had beaten Iowa 21–17 only after John Isenbarger, the punter, had tried to run instead of punt on fourth down, had failed, giving Iowa the ball for an easy go-ahead touchdown. A score in the last fifty-three seconds had saved the day. It had beaten Michigan 27–20 with a long drive in the last two minutes because Isenbarger had again tried to run instead of punt, allowing Michigan to tie the score. "Coach," Isenbarger had said. "Why do I *do* things like that?" Pont didn't know. And neither did Isenbarger's mother, who sent the halfback a wire which said, "Dear John. Please punt."

Indiana managed to beat Wisconsin only because

the Badgers were so inept. Trailing by only 14–9
with four minutes to play, Wisconsin proceeded to
drive toward the Hoosiers' goal. The Badgers got to
midfield. They got to the Indiana 30. They got to the
25. They shoved on to the 19. By now, the Indiana
defense looked about as organized as a hippie's crash
pad. On the sideline, John Pont poured hot coffee on
his wrist accidentally. Wisconsin got to the Indiana
10. There was time for one more play.

It was okay. John Isenbarger didn't have the ball.
A Wisconsin quarterback did. And he threw it over
the Indiana library, which was about a mile away.
The big red ball kept rolling.

CHICAGO, Illinois

The last of pro football's big spenders sauntered
into Soldier Field the other evening and masquer-
aded for a while in those blue jerseys with the red
stars on the shoulders as another illustrious squad of
College All-Stars. But the party didn't last long. As
they do every so often, the professional champions,
in this case the Green Bay Packers, got themselves
emotionally up for the occasion and buried the
rookies, all four million dollars worth, by the record
score of 38–0. The Packers were so efficient that the
game was obviously over by half time and realists in
the dark old edifice on Lake Michigan began to flee

to the lights of Rush Street, wondering once more if the annual mismatch is still necessary. It was perfectly clear that the collegians would rather have been in pro camp instead of wasting three weeks training for a contest that Donald Duck's nephews would have shown more interest in.

OXFORD, Mississippi

They had started coming at nine in the morning and parked in the Grove, the center of the Ole Miss campus. James Meredith wasn't there so it was all right. The old men raised the trunks of their cars and lifted out folding chairs, hammocks, tables, quilts and iceboxes. And whisky bottles. The women uncovered huge baskets of fried chicken and sandwiches. Young girls wiggled through the trees in their stiff hairdos, chewing gum and giggling. Young men looked at them and said, "Damned if I wouldn't tread a little water for that 'un over there." Children romped over the knolls. Couples played cards at the tables, read newspapers, or simply sweltered away in the ninety-three degree heat. Some slept. Some listened to the noises of the traffic confusion and wondered if the police were drinking coffee as usual in the school cafeteria, which they were. A man said, "Anybody who ain't started out from Memphis yet just ain't gonna make the kickoff."

This was William Faulkner's place on the day that another football season would begin.

NEW HAVEN, Connecticut

There stood this quarterback named Brian Dowling in the gangrened old Yale Bowl with his arm outstretched, upraised, a ball attached to the end of it, looking for all the world like the cover of the 1936 *Illustrated Football Annual.* Down the sideline, meanwhile, this big end was lumbering in the mud, head lowered, limbs rotating, as if he actually had faith that Dowling would throw the pass fifty yards over the clouds in these dwindling seconds to beat Harvard. And so, with what must have been a beautiful grunt, Dowling heaved the football. And then as it soared and soared, loyal Bulldogs in the wet and frozen throng surely must have had visions dancing through their heads of Bill Mallory and Bruce Caldwell, or of Albie Booth and Clint Frank. They were right. When the pass came down Yale had won a thing called The Game by 24–20, and suddenly everything was simply *maw*velous from Wall Street to Darien, give or take a few lockjaw accents.

DALLAS, Texas

It had always been the kind of game, said Darrell Royal, where you had to screw your navel to the ground. You had to scratch, bite and spit at the other guy all day long or he would have your lunch. This time would certainly be no different. It would be what Texas-Oklahoma games always are, the usual, according to Royal, "old-fashioned, country, jaw-to-jaw, knucks down gut check." Knucks down? Yeah, like when you shot marbles as a kid and then you started playing for "keeps," and everybody got knucks down. "You hoped that other guy's hand would quiver," said Royal, "and if it didn't, then you knew you were all covered up with trouble. We're all covered up with trouble against these people."

Texas was, but Texas is used to it. There had to be some reason why Royal's coaching record showed eleven victories and only two losses against the Sooners. In his bag of resources there was always the forward pass, and when Oklahoma seized a 14–0 lead, Royal once again had to call on it. So James Street started throwing and Cotton Speyrer started catching, and Texas won the state fair spectacle again by 27–17.

In some ways, these Texas-Oklahoma games are a bit much. Friday night before the game has become the biggest gut check of all, at least for the fans. For blocks, in the heart of the city, in the hours leading up to and just after midnight, the fans play something that could be called Saigon suburb. Sirens ring out as the city comes under siege of drunks, wanderers, shouters, pranksters, rooters and music makers. Only 475 got arrested this time, nowhere near the record. Well, maybe riots aren't what they used to be, but the Texas team is.

WEST LAFAYETTE, Indiana

Purdue University is the Big Ten's contribution to ethnic jokes. It is an arrangement of engineering textbooks, asphalt, and dull-red buildings on a Midwest plain, and through the years its football players have had such nicknames as Rail Splitters, Pumpkin Shuckers, Cedar Choppers, Blacksmiths, Hayseeds, Cornfield Sailors and Boilermakers. For a moment, consider the term Boilermakers, a derisive name Purdue *liked* and adopted officially. Does a Boilermaker sound like the kind of guy you would want your sister to date? Does he sound like *fun?* He's got to drive a '57 Buick, come from a family of fourteen in Gary, and spend his vacations breathing rivet dust. Yeah, yeah, he'll study for you and maybe become an astronaut — big deal — but he couldn't do the boogaloo if he loaded up on dexies, he couldn't find the Pump Room in Chicago with a compass, and he'd stumble on thick carpet. Naw, man. To have any class you've got to come from a cooled-out school like Wisconsin or Michigan or Northwestern. Pur-

due? Man, Purdue is like *Iowa*. After all, how many
Boilermakers do you know who can chew gum and
walk at the same time?

Well, there was at least one once named Bob
Griese. He might have been a farm-type lad from
Evansville, and he might have made the terrible
social mistake of going to Purdue, but put him in
Ross-Ade Stadium on a pale blue September day
against Notre Dame and he will bring out the Apoca-
lypse in you. Passing, running, kicking and thinking,
Bob Griese whooshed out the candlelight that Grantland Rice promised in the second and unremembered
paragraph of his Four Horsemen story would "always gleam through the Indiana sycamores." It
would in fact have taken all of the literary fame of
Harry Pestilence, Don Famine, Sleep Jim Destruc-
tion and Elmer War to have kept Griese from upsetting the Fighting Irish 25–21 in a grandly
melodramatic afternoon of football.

All Griese did was complete 19 of 22 passes for 283
yards and three touchdowns, run nine times for an
average of five yards per carry, punt three times
high, accurately and deliberately short to the Notre
Dame six, seven and twenty-six-yard lines, and make
a touchdown-saving tackle on defense. In the face of
such statistical goodies, and considering that they
came against a bitter and respectable enemy, Griese

left a lot of people wondering if they had ever seen a more brilliant performance by a quarterback.

The ironic thing was that Griese had wanted to attend Notre Dame but when he was preparing to visit South Bend an alumnus of the Fighting Irish told him the school wasn't interested because he was too small.

"I guess he had better remain anonymous," said Griese.

### DURHAM, North Carolina

The white caps of several more admirals had gone wheeling into the air over the deeds of Navy's Roger Staubach, and a countless number of Duke Blue Devils still lay winded on the field from chasing — and not catching — the most glamorous player of the year, but none of this seemed to matter much to an agate-eyed man named Wayne Hardin who happened to be Staubach's coach. Roger had given Navy its best team in decades and he was going to win the Heisman Trophy, but Hardin wanted it all kept a secret.

For several weeks, or ever since it appeared that Roger had a chance for the Heisman and Navy had a chance for a bowl bid and a lofty national rating, writers and photographers had been discouraged from trespassing on Annapolis ground. And now in

Durham they had been kept waiting outside the locker room for well over an hour since Staubach had won another game.

As I waited around I couldn't help remembering what Hardin had said earlier in the week. "More people would like to see Roger Staubach right now than any celebrity in the world," he said seriously. "If we opened the doors, do you have any idea how many writers and photographers would show up at our practice? It would be close to five thousand."

Presently the locker room door opened and a man came out wearing a crew cut like any other midshipman, but it wasn't Roger. It was Budd Thalman, the publicity man, who said softly that if we stood back a safe distance and stayed calm, he would produce "Rog."

Staubach finally walked out in his dress blues with his cap under his arm and blinked pleasantly while cameras clacked and everyone smiled at him. Wayne Hardin came out and lit a cigar. Thalman and Hardin stood on either side of the quarterback like presidential body guards. The interview lasted a wonderful eight minutes, and it went like this:

"Fine game, Roger," somebody said.

"Thanks."

"Were you worried out there for a while?"

"Sure was."

"Pretty tired?"

"Sure am."

"Guess you're looking forward to Army?"

"Beat Army," said Thalman.

"Sure am," said Staubach.

"Guess you take a lot of razzing from the team about your publicity, huh?"

"Sure do."

"Why are both of your knees taped during the games?"

"New style uniform," said Wayne Hardin. "If it goes over we'll put it on the market. Heh. Heh. Well, Rog, you're keeping forty-three other boys waiting on the bus."

A photographer moved in about three feet from Staubach, crouched down and aimed up for a portrait. Budd Thalman pressed his hand against the photographer's shoulder, smiled, wiggled his finger like a teacher telling a child he's been naughty and said, "Too close."

Staubach smiled and stood there.

"Forty-three other boys waiting, Rog. Let's go," said Hardin.

Staubach moved toward the bus but immediately got encircled by a group of youngsters asking for autographs. He began to sign for them. But the coach interrupted.

"Write the academy, boys," Hardin said. "We'll send you an autographed picture. Let's go, Rog."

With that, Roger Staubach disappeared into the custody of his keepers, not to reappear until another glorious Saturday.

Somebody once said that you can't win with the press. That the writers will always have the last word. I suppose it is true that most writers outlast all players and most coaches. Perhaps this is our reward. Perhaps this, more than anything else, is what this book is going to be about.

# 2

## Little Old Oaken Brown Jugs

*It's always more fun to play — and beat — somebody you know.*

No one has ever been able to figure out how old the sport of football is, except that it goes back at least two thousand years, which means that the Chinese may have invented it and therefore they also may have come up with the first traditional rivalry: the Hoys v. the Hos for possession of the Old Oaken Egg Roll, or something like that. What we do know is that Princeton and Rutgers played the first American version of the game back in 1869 and that even then as people watched from their frost-covered buckboards in New Brunswick, N.J., the collegiate sport had something extra that no other athletic endeavor would ever have — something that reached mysteriously beyond exercise for its own sake, love of competition, or, as the Chinese may have played it, most honorable shin splints.

That first game, of course, was hardly anything to compare with the slick perfection of the 1960's. It was twenty-five guys to a side removing their waistcoats and playing Kick the Groin with periodic time-outs to reinflate the pig bladder. Still, it furnished seeds for lasting contributions. Uniforms, for example: Rutgers wore red turbans. Cheers, for another example: Princeton's students gave the first football yell — some vague sort of chant they remembered from a few years earlier when New York's Seventh Regiment marched through town on its way to that great bowl game with the Confederacy. More important, however, Princeton and Rutgers initiated the custom of competing for more than the score.

The stake was a cannon. The Old Oaken Cannon? Well, no. It was just a Revolutionary War cannon that the two schools had been fighting over for a long time. The football game, they decided, would be a better way to determine who got it annually. After a few years Princeton got smart and cemented the relic in a bed of concrete, and this must have been the first football prank. But a point had been made. Football had tradition the moment it began.

Now skip a century. Leap over a pile of Walter Camps and Knute Rocknes — all of those men who have given sweep and technique to the game — and we come to a sport so colorfully aged by tradition and sustained by rivalries that a mere thirty million ticket buyers live and die with it every year regardless of who's No. 1, who's undefeated, who's All-America, or which Notre Dame player is winning another Heisman Trophy.

College football has become a geographical, historical and social event, and sometimes all three. Every fan has *somebody* he especially likes to see beaten. During the week of their game, Oshkosh feels about St. Norbert the way Army feels about Navy. Beneath the breast of every Michigan tuba player, it was once said, lies a hatred for Minnesota. Turn a UCLA man around three times and he'll stagger straight to the USC campus with a couple of buckets of blue and gold paint. Give a Texas oilman two drinks and he'll bet you every offshore well he's got (and some he hasn't got) that the Longhorns will whip Oklahoma.

Tradition and rivalry are words that belong almost exclusively to the vernacular of college football — right in there with Grange, Gipp, pursuit, three-deep, Harmon, Bear, Darrell, Roverback, O.J. and all that kind of thing. Old as the two words are, they are irreplaceable, for it is what they suggest that specifically separates the college game from that of the pros. Sophisticates, with their double drag-outs and their post-and-gos, may not like it, but college football *is* Michigan playing Minnesota for the Little

Brown Jug, a street brawl in downtown Dallas the night before the Texas-Oklahoma game, a thousand white Annapolis caps spraying into the air above Philadelphia's John F. Kennedy Stadium and that annual Wall Street Block Party and Raccoon Coat Parade known as the Yale-Harvard game.

There are many types of rivalries, all of which help any college season keep its hip pads up. There are intrastate rivalries, border rivalries, crosstown rivalries and interservice rivalries. These can be classed as natural rivalries. The most common, and perhaps by now the most overrated, are the intrastate rivalries. Any football-minded boy of seven can name the most noteworthy of them: Alabama-Auburn, Georgia-Georgia Tech, Purdue-Indiana, Tennessee-Vanderbilt, Michigan-Michigan State, Texas-Texas A&M, LSU-Tulane and so on; games which made popular that wonderful old notion, "Boy, you can throw out the record book when . . ."

In most cases today you can throw out the whole rivalry, because it has been replaced by something better. Major enemies have spread in college football like probation sentences. Sweet victories and sad upsets on both the conference and national levels tend to refocus the fan's attention.

Consistently good teams of long standing such as Notre Dame, Alabama, USC and Texas discover one day that their important rivals have not only changed but increased. For a time, Notre Dame's big games were with Army and USC. The Irish still have the Trojans, but they have added Michigan State and Purdue. USC also underwent a psychological shift: from Stanford and Cal in the old days to Notre Dame and UCLA today. In the South, Alabama and Tennessee would rather beat each other any day than Auburn and Vanderbilt, who are generally happy to beat anybody. And it has been thirty years since the Texas-Texas Aggie game has been as vital to its followers as the Oklahoma Saturday every October in Dallas, a contest that is college football's equivalent of a prison riot — with coeds. What has most helped these particular rivalries along is a rare season in which most of the teams involved are rated among the top twenty and how they fare against each other has a great deal to do with settling the national championship.

Meanwhile, a couple of fairly familiar schools named Yale and Harvard will play their game — *The Game,* so far as they're concerned — oblivious to anything as banal as the settling of a national championship in this day and time. They did that bit already.

Yale and Harvard compete in a league called the Ivy, the championship of which, they now claim, is important enough. If this is true for them, it is because they had a fifty-year head start on almost everybody else. The Crimson and the Bulldogs began playing football back in 1875; they were, one could say, the original traditional rivalry. Until the mid-1920's few teams outside of a small, select group of Eastern schools — Yale, Harvard, Princeton and Penn, mainly — ever impressed Walter Camp enough to gain a rating among his Big Four at the season's end. Walter Camp was the original AP poll.

One reason Yale and Harvard may have quit competing in the big time is that they grew weary of turning out legendary names, Yale, after all, produced Walter Camp himself, "the father of American football," who gave us the down system, the idea of eleven players to a side and modern scoring. Yale also produced Amos Alonzo Stagg, Pudge Heffelfinger, T.A.D. Jones, Ted Coy, Bill Mallory, Bruce Caldwell, Albie Booth, Larry Kelley and Clint Frank, along with an occasional Archibald MacLeish and John Hersey.

Harvard was just as busy. Coming out of Cambridge were the likes of Charles Daly, Hamilton Fish, Charlie Brickley, Eddie Mahan, Edward Casey, Barry Wood and a guard with the most perfect Ivy League name of all: Endicott Peabody. There were also a few Kennedys along the way. One of them, U.S. Senator Edward, scored Harvard's only touchdown in the 1955 loss to Yale.

Times have changed for The Game. Once the men who played were considered the noblest examples of manhood. There was nothing bestial about them. They were gentlemen of courage, bravery and daring who lured 70,000 into the Bowl at New Haven. A star was instantly taken into the social elite, and the old grads liked nothing better than to sit around the fires of their private clubs and dredge up memories of the day in 1913 when Charlie Brickley booted five field goals to beat Yale 15–5, or discuss, cut by cut, every scamper of Albie Booth.

Now it seems different. The nostalgic hero for today's students is more apt to be a man like Charlie Yeager, the Yale manager of 1952 who slipped into the game, as preplanned, to catch a pass for a conversion against poor Harvard. It is someone like the impulsive young girl in 1960 who dashed into the end zone to embrace Harvard's Charlie Ravenal as he scored his last touchdown in a rout. And it is someone like the Harvard student who arranged to let loose several greased pigs in the Yale Bowl during the 1953 game — and did.

For all of its deterioration as a game of importance to the outside world, there is still a color and an atmosphere to a Yale-Harvard weekend that few other rivalries can match. For example, there are intercollegiate competitions between the two schools on all levels — varsity, junior varsity and freshmen. There are also tackle games between all dorms. Thus, more than seven hundred students participate in football either Friday or Saturday, and there is soccer and touch football going on. It is difficult to walk down a street in either New Haven or Cambridge without being thrown a pass. And then on Saturday afternoon, between tailgate parties, with class reunions going on in candy-striped tents all over the parking lots, the two varsities get down to the more or less important business of the game . . . oops, The Game.

If Yale v. Harvard can best be described today as an intellectual rivalry, the Texas-Oklahoma game is just the opposite. It is raw, rugged and deadly serious. Fights frequently break out in the stands as well as on the field. It features some of the most aggressive hitting in the sport. At the moment of the kickoff the players are jumping up and down, as if they've swallowed something from the chemistry lab, and waving their arms in the manner of John Wayne leading his troops in a charge out of the trenches. The bands are simultaneously bursting forth with "The Eyes of Texas" and "Boomer Sooner," and more than 75,000 maniacs, pretty evenly divided, are

standing and screeching. This is fairly amazing, for
most of them are awfully hung over from the night
before when they just turned downtown Dallas into
a garage. Not so long ago a new record total of seven
hundred Texas and OU rowdies were jailed for dis-
turbing the peace in a No Man's Land known as the
corner of Commerce and Akard streets, a plot of
ground separating the Baker and Adolphus hotels
the evening before the big game.

While the Longhorns and Sooners have been playing since 1900 and while the game has been a special
attraction of the State Fair of Texas since 1915, it is
only since the end of World War II that the rivalry
has become intense.

What started it, aptly enough, was a near riot
during the 1947 game, which Texas won behind
Bobby Layne. A referee's decision caused several
thousand beverage bottles to be hurled down onto
the playing field — and the state fair has sold beer
and soft drinks in paper cups ever since. Then Oklahoma started to win the game too often under Bud
Wilkinson, sometimes winning it with prized recruits
from Texas. From 1948 through 1957, the Sooners
won nine of ten from Texas. This was during Oklahoma's glory days when Wilkinson coached five
undefeated teams and won three national championships. It was only after Texas hired Darrell Royal, a

former OU star, that things changed. Royal promptly won ten of twelve from Oklahoma. The ironies were obvious, and they added heat to a rivalry that would boil all on its own, thanks to memories of such confrontations as the 1963 game.

A year before Texas had won 9–6 and a gang fight between the two benches had been judged about a tie. Now, Oklahoma was No. 1, just like a few years earlier, but Texas was rated No. 2. The Cotton Bowl was a pandemoniacal sellout as always, with the usual number of people having tried to slip in at dawn and hide under benches or, as a drunk success-fully did in 1949, shinny up a light tower, hide and enjoy an aerial view of the game.

Among the '63 spectators was U.S. Senator Clinton P. Anderson from New Mexico, who sat among some OU fans. Early in the game the senator had to hear a lot about how Bud Wilkinson was going to win another national title this season, which would be his last, and then how easily Bud would win a U.S. Senate seat the following year in Oklahoma. When it was over, Texas had won 28–7, and it was Royal's team that was headed toward a national title. Filing out of the Cotton Bowl, Anderson told his OU friends, "That was the shortest term anyone ever spent in the U.S. Senate."

While it is understandable that Texas and Okla-

homa could have become such violent foes, being
close neighbors, it is not so easy to understand how
another august rivalry evolved: Michigan and Minnesota.

Geography certainly could not have had much to
do with it. Ann Arbor is closer to Nashville, Tenn.
than it is to Minneapolis. If you want the truth, the
Michigan-Minnesota thing for the Little Brown Jug
began by accident, although there is probably behind it some seed of the Midwestern ethic, a mutual
fondness for wheat fields, silos or duck hunting,
perhaps. At any rate, the Little Brown Jug, which is
neither little nor brown and never was, has become
football's best-known *objet d'art*, because Michigan
and Minnesota have played a lot of big games and
turned out hordes of good teams.

The jug, which is two and a half feet tall, was
originally an old gray plaster crock that Michigan
coach Fielding H. Yost carried around so that his
legions could drink fresh Ann Arbor spring water as
they went around beating everybody 60–0. The
tradition of Minnesota and Michigan playing for the
jug began with one of the most exotic upsets in
collegiate football history. It happened in 1903. That
year Michigan, with Willie Heston carrying the ball
to immortality, arrived in Minneapolis in the midst
of a memorable streak. The Wolverines had won 29

straight games, and had scored 1,631 points (56 per game) to a total of 12 for their opponents.

One of football's significant innovations took place that day. Minnesota used a seven man defensive line for the first time, with the other four players forming an early-day rendition of the umbrella secondary. Prior to this, all defenses had been nine-man lines (there was scarcely any passing), and Willie Heston had always been long gone every time he cracked through the first barrier. Minnesota's defense was designed to give him two walls to get through. He never did. Minnesota clawed its way to a 6–6 tie on old Northrup Field, and the only bigger news in 1903 was when Orville Wright did his thing a few weeks later at Kitty Hawk.

Yost and his team were in such a hurry to leave after the upset that they rushed off, forgetting the crock of water, which led to the immediate joke among Minnesota Swedes: "Jost left his *yug.*" The Gophers kept the jug and said Michigan would have to win it back. They have been fighting over it ever since. If the rivalry has improved with age, so has the jug. It is now painted maroon (for Minnesota) and blue (for Michigan), and the scores of all the games are on it.

The most famous modern contest for the jug came in 1940, a game that was the equivalent of the 1966

Notre Dame–Michigan State epic. Both teams were overstocked with stars. Michigan had Tom Harmon, who was busy breaking some of Red Grange's records. He would win the Heisman Trophy. The Wolverines also had four others who either were or would be All-Americas, one of them the noted blocking back Forest Evashevski. Michigan was undefeated in five games and went into Minneapolis, together with fifteen train cars of fans, as the No. 1 team. But Minnesota was just as undefeated, ranked No. 2 and had its own lineup of All-Americas, including tailback Bruce Smith, who would be the Heisman winner a year later, and a sophomore back named Bill Daley, who would lend a footnote to the series by becoming a *Michigan* All-America in 1943 when he wound up there through the fortunes of war and a naval training program.

There was only one thing wrong with what could have been as splendid a game as was ever played. It rained about four hundred million Little Brown Jugs full, turning the Minnesota stadium into the world's largest casserole. This hurt Michigan the most, for Harmon, who was fast and fancy, was slowed down to the speed of an arthritic climbing a staircase. He had a miserable afternoon, slipping and sloshing around and missing an extra point that still makes him irritable every time the subject comes up. He did pass for the touchdown that gave Michigan a 6–0 lead, but later on Bruce Smith, on a surprise reverse play, waded eighty yards for a touchdown and Minnesota became the national champion 7–6. Poor Tom, Old 98 he was called, still had a chance to win the game when he drove his team down to Minnesota's goal line in the fourth quarter. There, however, with a hole opened up for him as wide as his hometown of Gary, Indiana, Harmon slipped in the mud.

"I can still see the hole," Harmon would later say. "It's bigger than a room, but I just can't get there."

The most famous rivalry in all of sport is probably Army-Navy. It is a spectacle with the least provincial appeal of all, having a true national, even worldwide flavor. Battles have been interrupted — well, almost — because generals and admirals wanted to listen to the game around the globe on the Armed Forces Network. In fact, when Army completed an undefeated season in 1944 — the first of the Glenn Davis-Doc Blanchard teams — by beating Navy and sewing up No. 1, Army coach Red Blaik received the following telegram:

THE GREATEST OF ALL ARMY TEAMS STOP WE HAVE STOPPED THE WAR TO CELEBRATE YOUR MAGNIFICENT SUCCESS STOP

MACARTHUR

The game dates back to 1890. It was originated by a West Point cadet, Dennis Mahon Michie, after whom Army's stadium is named. Cadet Michie organized the game on the parade ground, and 500 people came out to watch halfback-coach-captain-manager-trainer Michie lead his team to a 24–0 loss. On the way to the game the Navy team had come across a goat it named Bill, and after Navy won, Bill was taken home to Annapolis as a mascot. The Midshipmen are now on their nineteenth Bill.

The series has been discontinued a couple of times because of anger. Very soon after it began, President Grover Cleveland stopped it. It seems that following the game of 1893, a brigadier general and a rear admiral got into such a bitter argument about it that they challenged each other to a duel. There was no Army-Navy game for five years.

The series was begun again only because of some wartime heroics. Four men who had played in the early games, including Dennis Michie, lost their lives in the Spanish-American War. The service academies decided that the men had gained much from their football experiences – they were better men and soldiers – and that the game could be resumed in this spirit.

The immense popularity of Army-Navy – it had the first ticket scalpers – caused it to go on the road.

Franklin Field in Philadelphia was the site for many
years, and now it has settled in Philadelphia's John
F. Kennedy Stadium, where more than 100,000 can
see it annually. It is the only college game that has
been on national television since the tube first
blipped.

The game could not have become an American
classic, of course, if the two academies had not
continually suited out interesting teams and played
some storybook contests. One particular game in
1926, before 110,000 in Chicago's Soldier Field, was
considered for years as "the greatest game ever
played." It was a 21–21 tie, with Navy's Tom Hamilton costarring with Army's Chris Cagle.

Upsets have been almost as thick as the gold braid
in the stands. Two of the most surprising came close
together, and they reflect the kind of respect the
institutions hold for each other. Army was undefeated in 1948 and Navy had not won a single game,
but the Midshipmen somehow managed a 21–21 tie.
Two years later Army was undefeated again, ranked
No. 1, and a four-touchdown favorite over a Navy
team that had won only two games, but Bob Zastrow
passed Navy to a 14–2 victory.

In between those two games, however, Army got
its revenge, and in more ways than one. Not only did
the Cadets whomp Navy 38–0, but they took advan-

tage of some espionage to embarrass the Midshipmen before all of their admirals. An Army officer on duty at Annapolis had learned of a Navy plan to hoist some banners poking fun at Army's 1949 schedule and to parody "On, Brave Old Army Team," the West Point fight song. Soon after both student bodies had done their usual pregame march-on, drills and salutes, they took their places across the field from each other and Navy cheerfully sang the parody:

> *We don't play Notre Dame.*
> *We don't play Tulane.*
> *We just play Davidson*
> *For that's the fearless Army way.*

Then the Midshipmen lofted a huge banner that said: *When Do You Drop Navy?*

Navy was mortified when the Army cheering section immediately unrolled a banner that said: *Today!*

Thinking this had to be coincidence, or incredible bad luck, the Middies quickly tried again with another of their banners. This one said: *Why Not Schedule Vassar?*

And Army countered with a sign that produced one of the biggest laughs Municipal Stadium ever heard. It read: *We Already Got Navy.*

A rivalry that produces nearly as many spectators

as Army-Navy every year, maybe even more pranks
and surely some of the best football, is that between
USC and UCLA. It is unique in one sense: two good
teams in the same town. The game was brought to
the full attention of the United States in 1967 when
the two schools battled for the national championship on television, and before 93,000 in the Los
Angeles Memorial Coliseum.

Since UCLA grew up to USC's stature in the
middle 1930's, the rivalry has become a social study.
It is USC, the stuffy private school, against UCLA,
the booming state institution. The two continuously
seem to be able to infiltrate each other's card cheering sections and mess up the messages, to paint
campus landmarks such as Tommy Trojan, to sabo-
tage bonfires, kidnap mascots, capture and punish
invaders, attempt bomb pranks and generally enjoy a
good old-fashioned collegiate hatred.

Since they are located in California's fantasyland,
both schools are naturally proud of all the celebrities
who have been a part of the series. USC likes to list
among its distinguished alumni an ex-tackle named
John Wayne, who was Marion Morrison in school;
the late Ward Bond, also a tackle; producer Aaron
Rosenberg, who was an All-America guard; All-
America halfback Cotton Warburton, who won an
Oscar in 1968 for film editing; and the noted TV

commentator, Frank Gifford. For background music, USC can point out that a fellow named Herb Alpert once marched in the Trojan band.

UCLA, meanwhile, has a list of its own that includes Mike Frankovich, an ex-quarterback who became the head of Columbia Pictures; actor Gary Lockwood, who was formerly a tackle named Gary Yurosek; and baseball's famed Jackie Robinson, who was a football hero first and a standout in one of the more memorable USC-UCLA games, the 0–0 tie of 1939.

The teams played eight games in the series before UCLA managed to win. That happened in 1942 when Bob Waterfield led the Bruins to their first Rose Bowl. If UCLA ever had a period when it slightly dominated the game it was during the late Red Sanders's time, 1949 through 1957, when his single-wing teams won six of nine from the Trojans. At that, he lost the big game they played in 1952, when both teams were unbeaten and untied and 97,000 stormed the Coliseum to see USC edge out a 14–12 victory.

A few years later, when John McKay got to USC and when Tommy Prothro took over at UCLA, the rivalry eased into a perfect dead-even matchup, one which could only keep serving thrill after thrill. In the first five games McKay and Prothro played as crosstown enemies — and not the best of personal friends — all were won and lost in the final minutes. Prothro, a big, serious man who smoked and drank Cokes incessantly, saw his teams capture the first two, 20–16 and 14–7. But McKay, a quick-witted, outgoing socializer, saw his Trojans swipe the next three by such melodramatic scores as 21–20 and 28–16 largely through the heroics of O. J. Simpson, and then by 14–12 on a desperation pass when all seemed lost.

When McKay was asked how he could stand up to such goings-on season after season, he remarked, "Because I've checked my heart and I don't have one."

National championships, titles, trophies, jugs, mugs and hugs — all of these are things that make up the game's traditional rivalries. It doesn't really matter if it's USC v. UCLA or hundreds of St. Olafs taking on hundreds of Carletons, for what is on display is the essence of a sport. No wonder the millions who thrive on college football like to think that it wasn't Columbus at all who discovered America. It was Princeton and Rutgers.

# 3

## The Alumni Cup

*Origins and quirks of America's favorite out-
rage — the fight for No. 1.*

**B**ACK in the days when college football players
wore those one-piece leather uniforms and
ran with the dazzling speed of tree trunks, it was
fairly easy to recognize the nation's No. 1 team every
season. Right there in *Harper's Weekly* or *Outing*
magazine you could see where this grizzled old noted
authority — Casper Whitney, say, or J. Parmly Paret
— had deciphered that either Yale, Harvard, Princeton or Penn had outgroped Columbia Law School
by the fattest margin, and he boldly proclaimed them
the mythical national champion. Nobody argued
about it, preoccupied as most people were with
striking for an eight-hour workday. Nobody even
cared. You told a friend that your school was No. 1
in those days and all he said was, "Listen, that's

great. But excuse me. I've got to go invent the air-
plane."

Things have certainly changed a lot since those
quiet days, of course, as surely everyone who has
ever been caught in a stadium traffic jam must know.
Today there is hardly any crusade in sport which can
equal the quest of the fan, coach or player for No. 1.
It is the holiest of grails in college football, and "the
alumni cup," as coaches have come to refer to any
kind of national championship — there never having
been any form of championship playoff — has become a symbol of the overall passion that surrounds
the game.

Football has been America's idea of the lions v. the
Christians for a long time and, as competitive and
success-seeking as we are, it was probably only natural that we would come up with something as out-
raging and at times as insanely opinionated as rating
systems which would insinuate that one school was
tougher — classier, speedier, smarter, better *bred* —
than another. So say psychologists.

I must confess that I have been in a football
stadium every Saturday more often by choice than
by duty for more than thirty years, and will assure
anyone who is uncertain about it that there is no
drama, suspense, excitement, thrill or feeling of ne-

cessity in sport that can equal the countdown to an
opening kickoff between two great teams or conten-
ders for that elusive, cantankerous, agonizing, dread-
ful and wonderful thing called No. 1.

A good example of how far the madness has pro-
gressed came in 1966 when there was blood spilled
all over such well-known venues of the game as
South Bend, Indiana, East Lansing, Michigan, and
Tuscaloosa, Alabama, about which team, by God,
was No. 1. Just as the decisions were about to be
made by all of the people who by now were choosing
national champions — everyone, it seemed, from the
AP to Sara Lee — Notre Dame and Michigan State
upped and played a 10–10 tie, dislodging one
another from perfect records. Alabama, then, which
was the other serious contender, continued on undefeated and untied through a bowl game. But when
the final polls were released Notre Dame had won by
the length of Coach Ara Parseghian's name. Five of
the seven most respectable award-givers, AP, UPI,
the Football Writers, Dick Dunkel and Frank
Litkenhous liked the Fighting Irish despite their tie
with the Spartans. The other two, the Hall of Fame
and the Helms Athletic Foundation, settled on a tie
of their own between Notre Dame and Michigan
State. So what did Alabama do? Well, the loyal
friends of Bear Bryant went out and put license

plates on their automobiles which said: TO HELL WITH
AP AND UP, ALABAMA IS NO. 1.

As it happened, I learned rather early in life that
the result of a college football game was more important than wars or depressions. I learned it at the first
college game I ever attended which was three days
before my seventh birthday on the contemptuous
afternoon of November 30, 1935. This was the day of
the biggest thing that ever happened to Fort Worth,
Texas, a game between TCU (11–0) and SMU
(11–0) to see who got the Rose Bowl bid. My father
has never revealed how he got us the tickets, which
went for $100 each, but getting to go to the game
was my birthday present.

Now, of course, all I knew at the time was that it
was an event of some vital interest around the house-
hold. Only later would I discover how immense it
was, with Bill Stern and Grantland Rice and all such
celebrities as that coming down for it. I would remember that there were more people than I had ever
seen before in, around, outside of, down on the field
of, and trying viciously to get into, the stadium. The
grandstands at TCU in those days held only 24,000,
and the best estimate is that maybe 40,000 somehow
got in, largely by driving their cars through the wire
fence that surrounded the place.

I recall that we arrived two or three hours before

the kickoff and that my father, a long-suffering TCU fan who *still* hasn't recovered from that game, bought and pinned on me a huge purple and white button with a picture of a player on it and printing which said: I AM FOR SLINGIN' SAM BAUGH AND THE FIGHTIN' FROGS.

Well, it was one hell of a game, as many historians know, with SMU taking a 14–0 lead and then TCU tying it up 14–14, and then SMU winning 20–14 in the last minutes when some of Sam Baugh's desperate passes were dropped. I didn't appreciate it, naturally. What intrigued me more than anything were the uniforms, which I thought were really nifty. TCU wore polished black leather helmets and white jerseys with a silken glaze to them on which were large purple numbers. They wore khaki pants that had a golden hue in the sunlight, and there were sleek purple stripes down the backs of them. Ah, but SMU. The Mustangs' helmets were bright blue and so were their shirts. And their pants were bright blue and bright red.

"SMU's suits really look keen," I said.

"You don't know what you're talkin' about," my Dad said.

I did realize that TCU didn't win the game, but it was a few years later before I understood why my father and I, and some of his friends, sat there for two hours after it was over while they all had misty eyes and used some funny language and kept taking swigs out of these little silver-looking bottles in their pockets. "Cough medicine," my Dad said it was, but when I coughed he said I didn't need any.

Anyhow, that whole experience told me exactly how important college football was.

The thing that has contributed so much interest to delirious fall Saturdays like the one I have tried to describe is something called the Poll. Surprisingly, it is not nearly so ancient as the naming of the "intercollegiate champion" by Casper Whitney or J. Parmly Paret. Ironically, it can be traced back only as far as — naturally — good old Knute Rockne at good old Notre Dame.

What occurred was this. In 1926 a teacher of economics at the University of Illinois named Frank G. Dickinson was a football buff who privately enjoyed rating all of the teams in the country by his own mathematical formula. He happened to mention this in the classroom one day and a student on the back row who was sports editor of the *Daily Illini* wrote a story about it. The story came to the attention of a Chicago clothing manufacturer named Jack Rissman, another buff, who decided he would like to use Dickinson's ratings to select the top team in the Big Nine (later Ten, of course) each year — they didn't all play each other — so that he could present a trophy to the winner. When Rockne heard about this, he invited both the professor and Rissman to lunch at South Bend and said, "Why don't you make it a national trophy that Notre Dame will have a chance to win?" Never one to miss out on a good thing, Rockne also persuaded Dickinson and Rissman to predate the whole thing a couple of years so that the 1924 Fighting Irish, the Four Horsemen team, could be the first truly "official" national champion.

This was actually how polls began, and how Notre Dame won its first national title. At lunch.

For better or for worse, Dickinson's system was relatively simple. At the end of the season he divided all teams into two categories — those that won more games than they lost, and those that didn't. He then awarded points for victories over teams in the first division and fewer points for victories over teams in the second division. Quality of schedule was not a factor but, just as inequitably, the number of games played was, except for bowls. Still, the Dickinson system was accepted by football fans as the law until well into the 1930's. By then there was a glut of other systems.

The next one followed Dickinson by about a year. It was perfected by a man named Deke Houlgate in

Los Angeles who would later write a 9 × 13 work titled *The Football Thesaurus*. Houlgate freely admitted that his system was devised to counter the "Midwest sectionalism" of Dickinson's. Houlgate's system, so far as anyone could tell, was his own personal opinion.

Next to come was a snappy thing called "Azzi Ratem" in 1928 by a man named William F. Boand. His selections were published annually in the *Illustrated Football Annual*, a highly regarded fan magazine. Like Dickinson, Boand predated his choices back to 1924. Curiously, for the 1937 edition Boand went back thirteen seasons and rerated the top teams, taking bowl results into consideration and then pronounced the list official.

The syndicated experts came on the scene in 1929 with the emergence of Dick Dunkel's "power index." Paul Williamson, a geologist by profession and a member of the Sugar Bowl committee, began his widely accepted "power ratings" in 1932. And Frank Litkenhous and his brother Edward started the "difference-by-score" method in 1934. Aside from their not overly revealing names, the details of how these systems work have remained a close secret, closely guarded by the various inventors.

Perhaps a bit irritated by the flood of experts on the scene who had never coached football, Parke H.

Davis, the most notable historian the game has known, decided to set all the records straight in the 1934 edition of *Spalding's Football Guide*. A member of Princeton's tug-of-war team in 1889, a former coach at Wisconsin, Amherst and Lafayette, and then a lawyer, Davis almost went back to the first inflated pig bladder and picked the national champions for every season, often settling for a variety of ties. Davis used no special method. He simply looked at the schedules and the results and chose his winners, give or take a few mild prejudices.

And now it was time for the popularity polls to begin. The first of these was that of the Associated Press, which started in mid-season of 1936. It still works the same way. Around fifty writers and broadcasters in the country whose organizations subscribe to AP are asked each week to vote on their top ten teams. The poll has splendid prestige but of course it is no more reliable than the insular tendencies of those who vote.

Our other wire service, United Press International, started its poll in 1950 but rather than rely on journalists, the UPI originated a board of college coaches. Thirty-five of them. It too has gained respect, but a lot of coaches have confessed that they often vote for forthcoming opponents or for teams from their own areas.

In between the two wire services' polls, in 1948, the Helms Athletic Foundation decided to name a national champion. It also chose to pore back through the years, as Parke H. Davis had done, and select past champions. The director of Helms since its beginning, Bill Schroeder, did the paper work, and he still heads the committee that picks the No. 1 team every season after the bowls. "A committee of one — me," he told me.

Because of their discontent with *all* polls, especially those of the wire services, the Football Writers Association of America set about naming the national champion in 1954. But if anyone thinks the association's 1,200 members have anything to do with it, they can guess again. Only five men decide the winner, a national panel — very secret — that is named by whoever happens to be president.

The most recent group to bequeath an alumni cup is the National Hall of Fame, which began circulating the MacArthur Bowl in 1959. It also picks the national champion by committee. Although the results don't reflect it, the committee is Eastern oriented, and it has the extra pressure of having to stage a formal dinner at the Waldorf every year at which the coach of the No. 1 team is a feature attraction.

This covers the origins and quirks of our national polls, but it doesn't say all there is to be said for them. I leave that to some of the victims in the coaching business.

John McKay: "All I know is that John McKay reads them, my kids read them, and everyone I know reads them. They must create a little interest."

Bear Bryant: "I know and our fans know that any year Alabama isn't up there trying to be Number One, the coach has done a sorry job."

Duffy Daugherty: "They only mean your good health and your future security."

Darrell Royal: "I'd like to think they're accurate because we've won a couple. But in the Southwest we all stay pretty depressed until we're still unbeaten and Notre Dame and everybody in the Big Ten has been knocked off."

What is available to the reader in the appendix of this book is the first complete and wholly accurate list ever compiled of college football's mythical national champions. It is also the *only* list. Every recognized authority that ever presumed to name a No. 1 is included. The selections date back to 1889, just twenty years after the birth of the American game. This was also a year distinguished by the first appearance of All-America teams.

The selectors represented are the Parke H. Davis Ratings (1889–1935), the Helms Athletic Foundation (1889–1969), the Dickinson System (1924–

1940), the *Illustrated Football Annual* (1924–1941), *The Football Thesaurus* (1927–1958), the Dunkel System (1929–1969), the Litkenhous System (1934–1969), the Williamson System (1932–1963), the Associated Press (1936–1969), the United Press International (1950–1969), the Football Writers Association of America (1954–1969), and the National Football Hall of Fame (1959–1969).

Only the most persistent historian would be able to gather such material. Easily obtainable are the AP, UPI, Football Writers, Hall of Fame and Helms records. Indeed, most modern record books include them. For Dunkel, Litkenhous and Williamson, however, one must pore through back issues of daily newspapers which have subscribed to these services. For Dickinson, one must contact Dickinson himself. In order to acquire the *Illustrated Football Annual* list, one must at least own a copy of the 1937 edition, plus the five editions which followed. And, finally, only a tattered old copy of the 1934 *Spalding Football Guide* will supply you with Parke H. Davis's selections.

The chart appendix tells us an awful lot about our maddening pursuit of No. 1. A number of statistical games can be played with it, and I have played most of them.

For instance, a careful count reveals that in all of

history only forty-two teams have claimed some kind of national championship, however prominent or remote. This is not very many, considering that more than 200 schools have at one time or another been considered major teams and were therefore in the running.

It turns out further that only twenty-eight schools have managed to win two national championships. And as we carry the idea onward, only twenty-three have been rewarded three times and only seventeen have captured four of them.

For easy reference to settle arguments with, here is a breakdown on the twenty-eight teams that have won at least two No. 1's:

| | | | | | |
|---|---|---|---|---|---|
| 1. | Notre Dame | 14 | 15. | Cornell | 4 |
| 2. | Yale | 13 | 16. | Illinois | 4 |
| 3. | Princeton | 12 | 17. | Tennessee | 4 |
| 4. | Alabama | 8 | 18. | Iowa | 3 |
| 5. | Harvard | 8 | 19. | Oklahoma | 3 |
| 6. | Pittsburgh | 8 | 20. | Lafayette | 3 |
| 7. | USC | 8 | 21. | LSU | 3 |
| 8. | Michigan | 7 | 22. | Ole Miss | 3 |
| 9. | Ohio State | 6 | 23. | Texas | 3 |
| 10. | Minnesota | 6 | 24. | California | 2 |
| 11. | Penn | 6 | 25. | Chicago | 2 |
| 12. | Army | 5 | 26. | Georgia | 2 |
| 13. | Ga. Tech | 5 | 27. | Maryland | 2 |
| 14. | Mich. State | 5 | 28. | Stanford | 2 |

To be a national champion is one thing, but to be a unanimous national champion is quite something else, of course. Especially considering the wholesale eruption of selectors in the modern era.

It happens that in all of the eighty years of selections, only twenty-six teams were designated as unanimous choices. On close inspection, we find Yale with five, Princeton and Harvard with three apiece, and only Notre Dame, Texas, Army and Penn with two each. The others are Oklahoma, Georgia Tech, USC, Michigan, Illinois, Pittsburgh and Ohio State.

The greatness of a golfer can be measured by the number of major championships he has won — a Masters, a U.S. Open or a British Open, that sort of thing — and in the same way we can measure the greatness of a college football coach by the number of No. 1 trophies that he gathered.

Well, exactly thirty-seven men throughout the history of the American game have been fortunate enough to see their teams win at least two such awards. The leader of them all doesn't happen to be Knute Rockne or Walter Camp or even Bear Bryant, as the world might automatically assume. He happens to be Howard Jones.

Jones holds a fascinating number of distinctions aside from the fact that he brought a special kind of fame to the Trojans of Southern California. He was, first of all, one of only four coaches who won a national championship at more than one campus. The others were Jock Sutherland who took his first at Lafayette and then bagged five more at Pitt, Pop Warner who won twice at Pitt and then got another at Stanford, and Fritz Crisler who got two at Princeton and then added a third at Michigan.

But Howard Jones outdid them all. He coached Yale to the title in 1909, then moved on to Iowa to take another in 1921, and then he really got started at USC where he took his other six, the last coming in 1939 — precisely thirty years after his first.

Regardless of who is and who isn't in the Hall of Fame, the true geniuses of coaching have been, to my mind, these gentlemen who have dominated the wild pursuit of the elusive No. 1. And it seems to be in order about now to list those special few who have been honored by two national championship teams or more. In no particular order where ties are concerned, they are:

| | | | |
|---|---|---|---|
| Howard Jones | 8 | Bob Zuppke | 4 |
| Jock Sutherland | 6 | Bill Roper | 4 |
| Knute Rockne | 5 | Bud Wilkinson | 3 |
| Frank Leahy | 5 | Bear Bryant | 3 |
| Bernie Bierman | 5 | Red Blaik | 3 |
| Woody Hayes | 4 | Bobby Dodd | 3 |
| Bob Neyland | 4 | Fritz Crisler | 3 |

| | | | |
|---|---|---|---|
| Johnny Vaught | 3 | Ara Parseghian | 2 |
| Wallace Wade | 3 | Biggie Munn | 2 |
| Duffy Daugherty | 3 | Jim Tatum | 2 |
| Pop Warner | 3 | Fielding H. Yost | 2 |
| Percy Haughton | 3 | Forest Evashevski | 2 |
| George Woodruff | 3 | Amos Alonzo Stagg | 2 |
| Darrell Royal | 2 | Charley Daly | 2 |
| John McKay | 2 | Harry Kipke | 2 |
| Walter Camp | 2 | Frank Thomas | 2 |
| Wally Butts | 2 | Bernie Moore | 2 |
| Gil Dobie | 2 | Bill Rhodes | 2 |

Comes now an incredibly select group, this being those coaches who have won *two unanimous* national championships. A man would lose a lot of money betting on the obvious — the Rocknes or Wilkinsons or Bryants or Neylands. Or even betting on Howard Jones. It so happens that only five men have achieved this goal and they span practically the entire history of the game.

The exclusive club includes the following: Walter Camp at Yale in 1891 and 1892, Percy Haughton at Harvard in 1910 and 1912, Red Blaik at Army in 1944 and 1945, Frank Leahy at Notre Dame in 1943 and 1949, and Darrell Royal at Texas in 1963 and 1969.

I have discovered that people who take a deep interest in all such lore and statistics of football can get so caught up in the mystique of the game that they no longer speak English.

The dawning of every season gives them a new vocabulary. You would never know today that all you had to do to be considered an ardent follower of football at one time was ride around in a jalopy and give an occasional locomotive for Jack Oakie, or maybe listen to Bill Stern, or know what "hike" meant.

Many of my friends now talk like coaches. They refer to a player being able to stick you or outbutt you. They think they see fly guys running post and flag patterns and doing down-and-ins, hitch-and-goes and zig-outs to the complete bewilderment of free safeties. They pretend to know an I-Slot formation and a Shifting-T, a Homer's Triple and the Veer. They watch monsters play the fat side.

They are certain they can read a blitz, storm, dog, blow, shoot, come, go or rain, and they know the linebackers who do this by such names as Mike (middle), Wanda (weak) and Sarah (strong).

They say that a broken field runner who is any good will give it to you and take it away; that he has a minuet in him; that a fast one is a streak who'll blow it across the alumni stripe.

They say a good passer is one who can press the button or hang it up there for six or put it in the seams. Especially if he has a receiver with good boards who doesn't hear footsteps.

What is involved in such shoptalk, and behind all of this lore, is the essence of a sport that has become a religion to millions. No. 1 is always going to be out there somewhere just a bit out of reach for most, but it will always provide a rather magnificent dream for the whole.

Obviously the game has hooked me as much as anyone you know. Perhaps more so. I know that the thought of being paid to watch football games was the thing that first made me want to own a typewriter, and then to enter into a profession that Red Smith always said was a lot better than working for a living.

But any time I catch myself thinking that football is *too* important, I try to remember what John McKay once told his Trojans at USC before a terribly big game, hoping to loosen them up.

"I won't try to tell you that this game isn't immense," said John. "But we ought to keep in mind that there are over six hundred million Chinese who don't care whether we win or lose."

# 4

## The Disciples of Saint Darrell

*A wild weekend with fans who like their foot-
ball in Stetson-sized doses.*

**O**N a bright, warm Friday morning one fine October down in Texas, a man named Elbert Joseph
Coffman woke up with a squirrel in his stomach. In
his good life as an outrageous football fan there had
never been a weekend quite like the one coming up.
In the next fifty-five hours or so he was going to see
three big college games and one pro game, and the
excitement of it all, the importance of the games,
made him nervous. Nervous but delighted. Football
to Joe Coffman, and thousands of other Texans, had
always been as essential as air conditioning. It was
what a Texan grew up with, fed on, worshipped,
followed, played, and, very often, died with. So it
was that Joe Coffman, thirtyish, married, father,
businessman, University of Texas graduate, football

incurable, was either going to live a lot this weekend — or die a little.

The first game, SMU against Navy, would be
played that evening in the Cotton Bowl in Dallas,
just thirty-five miles away from Joe Coffman's home
in Fort Worth. The next day he would go back to the
same stadium to see the biggest one of them all,
Oklahoma, ranked first in the country, against Texas,
ranked second. He would drive to Waco (ninety
miles south) Saturday night to watch Baylor
against Arkansas. And on Sunday he would return to
the Cotton Bowl to see the NFL's Dallas Cowboys
play the Detroit Lions.

If Joe Coffman's schedule seemed arduous, it was
little more so than that of many others in the state.
Thousands less fortunate than Coffman in getting
tickets to the big games would settle for a game or
two on television and radio and perhaps see a couple
of high schools play. But Joe Coffman also knew that
there would be more to his weekend than football.
He knew that it was going to cost him at least $200,
that he would be running into old friends, that there
would be as many parties as kickoffs and that he
would probably consume as much beer as might
have been served in a London pub on V-E day. But
Joe Coffman had been waiting months for this weekend and, as he prepared to leave home for his office

at the business he owned near downtown Fort Worth, the only thing that concerned him was whether everybody was as ready as he was. Everybody included Joe's wife, Mary Sue, another couple, Pat and Cecil A. Morgan Jr. (he was a stockbroker and a former University of Texas basketball star), and the Coffmans' baby-sitter. "I'll tell you one thing, Mary Sue," said Joe. "We got to be suited up and ready to go by five o'clock. We're gonna be in Dallas by six or I'm gonna raise more hell than the alligators did when the pond went dry."

Joe Coffman was a modern Texan. This meant that Mary Sue was a pretty, loving and understanding wife, that his sons Bobby, six, and Larry, four, were healthy and happy, that his business was successful (four other branches in Austin, San Antonio, Lubbock and Amarillo), that his ranch-type home was comfortable, with all of the built-ins manufacturers sell these days, that he had an Oldsmobile Starfire and an Impala (both convertibles), that his close friends were mostly the ones he grew up with or knew in high school and college. Being a modern Texan also meant that Joe Coffman might not recognize a cow pony if it were tied on a leash in his backyard, that he despised Stetson hats, that he liked cashmere sports coats, pin-collar shirts, Las Vegas, playing golf at Colonial Country Club, Barbra

Streisand ("Think she can't sing?"), good food, good booze, Barry Goldwater and, more than anything else, the Texas Longhorns. And did he like those Longhorns?

"They got too much character to lose that game," Joe said about Texas as he browsed through the mail on his desk at the office, drank some coffee and talked on the phone. Like any loyal Longhorn, his preoccupation with the OU game was all-consuming. The other games, they were good ones, Joe Coffman felt, but his good health, he said, his well-being and welfare would be riding with the Longhorns. It was not a very good day for work.

"I got to think a Bloody Mary's the answer," he said, heading out to Colonial Country Club. There would be friends there, talking football, "getting down" (making bets), and the time would pass more quickly through the endless football arguments that take place in Colonial's nineteenth hole the day before the games.

"Hey, Coffman," someone called as Joe entered Colonial and headed toward a table. "What are the Sooners gonna do to those T-sippers?" Joe Coffman removed his sunglasses, postured with his fist raised like Mussolini and said, "We're gonna send them sumitches back across the Red River, boys." He greeted a table of friends, ordered drinks and replied to every argument about the strength of Oklahoma's team with his message of the week: "Have to win, boys. Too much character. We got too much character to lose that game." Several Bloody Marys later, Joe Coffman had got through the day. Now the long, exhausting — and utterly perfect — weekend began.

It is roughly thirty-five miles, or twenty-five minutes, by way of the toll road from Fort Worth to Dallas. The first stop on Friday night for Mary Sue and Joe Coffman and Pat and Cecil Morgan was Gordo's. Gordo's was to Dallas what the Cafe Select was to *The Sun Also Rises*. It was a tiny beer-pizza-steak-sandwich parlor across from the SMU campus. Through its portals strolled many of Dallas's prettiest girls, its brawniest athletes, its newspaper columnists, flacks, poets, politicians and everyone, in fact, who was in enough to know about the place or who liked the world's best pizza or steak sandwich or who wanted Gordon West, the owner, to cash a personal check.

The dilemma of the visitor to Gordo's was what to eat. "I got to have a steak sandwich and a cheeseburger between two pizzas," said Joe. "It's all so good, I can't stand it."

Mary Sue, a small blonde who went two years to SMU and then graduated from Texas, suggested that whatever they were to have they have it quickly, because the traffic to the Cotton Bowl for the SMU-Navy game was going to be pretty brutal.

"I hope SMU does good," she said. "Do they have a chance to beat Navy, Joe?"

"Flattop Fry, boys," said Joe in his sepulchral voice, as if he had been asked to answer the entire room.

"Old Flattop," said Cecil Morgan. It was Joe and Cecil's private way of making fun of SMU's crew-cut coach Hayden Fry, who somehow acquired that nickname from them. Coffman and Morgan, given time, can make fun of every coach in the country — except Texas's Darrell Royal.

"Can they, Joe?" Mary Sue asked.

"Hell, yes," said Joe. "They haven't got any athletes, but they'll get after 'em. Like to see it. Be the start of an upset weekend, boys. The one we gotta have is tomorrow, though. Got to send 'em back across the Red River." Joe ordered another beer. And another. And one more.

"We better move out," Cecil Morgan said presently. "They're gonna hang us up in that state fair traffic."

"Yawl want paper cups?" Gordo asked, thoughtfully.

"I 'magine," said Joe. "Take that pizza with you, Mary Sue. Grab that beer, Cecil. We got to go see the Red Helmets play the Navys."

"Old Flattop," said Cecil.

There is no easy way to reach the Cotton Bowl in Dallas except to be dropped into it by helicopter. The stadium sits squarely in the middle of the Texas State Fairgrounds, and all roads lead in confusion from downtown Dallas about two miles away. That week the fair was in full swing. Indeed, that was the reason for three games in three days. It was almost as though somebody said, "There's no use bringin' 'em in from halfway 'cross the state for one li'l ol' extravaganza." Complaining about the traffic and the parking at the Cotton Bowl has always been one of Dallas's favorite pastimes. It is not so amusing when one wants to make a kickoff.

Behind the wheel of his Starfire, Joe Coffman sighed, "Man, man. Only stadium in the whole world where you have to get here on Wednesday to make a Friday night game."

Mary Sue said, "I can't believe all these cars are going to the SMU game."

"They aren't," said Cecil. "They're goin' to buy balloons. I'll guarantee you, there's seven million people out here tonight to buy balloons."

"Main thing they're doing," said Joe, "is driving in front of me."

By the time they had reached a parking place inside the state fairgrounds and trudged through the dust of the carnival midway, with only one beer stop, and then reached their seats, the game was five minutes old.

"Look at that!" Joe said, pointing at the SMU bench. "Flattop Fry don't know how many players he can send in or take out. He just sends in ten men every time."

"Saint Darrell knows the rules," said Cecil.

"I 'magine," said Joe.

As the SMU-Navy game wore on, it became clear that SMU was in no mood to lose as easily as the odds (thirteen points) had suggested. In fact, by the start of the fourth quarter Joe and Cecil had become enraptured with SMU's blazing-fast sophomore, tailback John Roderick, whose running was exciting them more than the passing of Navy's Roger Staubach. Although there merely as impartial observers, saving their enthusiasm for the Longhorns, Joe and Cecil could not resist blending themselves into the madness of the occasion as SMU won rather miraculously 32–28. The wives, Mary Sue and Pat, might have enjoyed it more if they had not been so fascinated by the conversation of an elderly Dallas lady in front of them, who kept talking to a friend about the "common people from Fort Worth."

Once Mary Sue giggled to Joe, "You can't believe what this woman is saying. She's saying that no saleswoman in Dallas will wait on Fort Worth people because they come over here without hats or gloves on. Just common as can be, she said." Joe roared. He leaned down the aisle and repeated it to Cecil. Cecil roared. It gave them a theme for the weekend, and some exit lines from the stadium.

"Naw," said Cecil, "we jest gonna git our common little ol' wives and go git drunked up on thet ol' beer."

"Good Lord, Cecil," said Pat. "You sound country enough without talking that way."

"Hell, we jest common," Joe laughed. He looked at Cecil. "You 'bout half country, ain't you, boy?"

They were badly in need of a beer.

"It'd be gooder'n snuff," said Cecil as Pat frowned, and they walked to the parking lot.

The Friday night before the annual Texas-OU game is a night that Dallas must brace for all year long.

Even without another football game to further overcrowd the city, which considers itself a cultural oasis in a vast wilderness of oil workers' helmets and

Levi's, the downtown area is declared off limits by every sane person, cultured or not. Throngs of students and fans gather in the streets, whisky bottles sail out of hotel windows, automobiles jam and collide and the sound of sirens furnishes eerie background music to the unstill night. Joe Coffman skillfully managed to commit his group to a post-SMU-game party (or pre-Texas-OU-game party) in the cultural suburbs, where the status symbols are a lawn of St. Augustine grass and a full-growing mimosa tree.

"Joe, are all of those funny people really going to be there?" Mary Sue asked as they drove out the Central Expressway.

"Honey, I got no idea. All I know is, they said come on out and they'd give a man a drink. And I know a man who really wants one."

"What's the name of the apartments?" Pat asked.

"I got the address," said Joe. "That's all. It's one of those Miami-Las Vegas names. Every apartment in Dallas, I'll guarantee you, sounds like a Polynesian drink. The Sand and Sea, or the Ski-Sky-You, or something."

"I think it's The Antigua," said Cecil.

"Well," said Joe, "that figures."

Through the night the party was both visible and

audible before Joe parked the car. People were
standing on the lawn, sitting on the steps of other
apartment units or gathered around a clump of trees.
The door was open. A Ray Charles record poured
out. Inside there was a curious mixture of "stewardi,"
as Joe described the girls, along with SMU fans,
Texas fans, Oklahoma fans, Dallas Cowboy fans,
Dallas Cowboys, bartenders, musicians, entertainers
from the city's private clubs, models and artists.

Joe observed the crowd and turned to Cecil and
said, "Go any*whur,* do any*thang.*" And they inched
toward the bar. Joe saw a man he had been with in
the Army. Mary Sue saw a girl friend she was supposed to have met at the game. Cecil calmly studied
the wall. On it were a Columbia pennant, a bizarre
unidentified animal's head with a sign hanging
around it that read, "Joe Don Looney," a bullfight
poster and a drawn sign that proclaimed, "If the
Lord Didn't Want Man to Drink, He Wouldn't Have
Give Him a Mouth." In the bathroom hung a replica
of the Mona Lisa. Joe saw an old fraternity buddy
from Austin, an SAE. "Sex Above Everything," said
Joe, shaking hands. Somebody said Henny Young-
man had been there but left because nobody wanted
to talk to him. Somebody said strippers were coming
over from the Carousel club. A man who kept intro-

ducing himself as "Sandy Winfield" and "Troy Donahue" said it had not turned out to be a bad party, considering he had not called anyone. No one ever found out who lived in the apartment.

Joe Coffman was making coffee at home by seven o'clock Saturday morning on four hours' sleep. He stared blankly at the Fort Worth morning *Star-Telegram*, which had the starting lineups for the Texas-OU game, and said, half to his sons and half to the western world, "They outweigh us, but we got too much character." By nine o'clock he was dressed and ready, except for his lucky cuff links. "Tell you one thing, honey," he said. "If I can't find my cuff links, there's gonna be more hell raised than there are Chinamen." Mary Sue went to a drawer and got them. "You just won the game," said Joe.

Everything moved briskly now. Joe took one son, Bobby, to a party, and arranged for him to get home. Cecil called and said he was on the way with the car already gassed up and the beer iced down. Joe told him the sitter was due about the same time. It was Eva Mae, he said. "All I know is, she's the head pie lady at Paschal High. Bakes twenty to thirty a day." They hung up, laughing. The two couples were on the road at 10:00 A.M.

Cecil was plugging along nicely on the toll road when Pat reminded him that he was going eighty mph. The speed limit was seventy.

"Can't get there too soon," said Joe. "Got to hear Hank Thompson. He's always singing on the fairgrounds at noon."

"Yeah," said Cecil. "That's about like you common people from Fort Worth. You *lack* them hillbilly *sangers.*"

Said Joe, "Can't beat it. Drink beer, listen to old Hank and then warp the Okies. Perfect day. I had to have about fifty dollars worth of that five and a half points."

"Did you bet, Joe?" said Mary Sue in a concerned voice.

"I 'magine."

Mary Sue looked out of the window.

"We're gonna warp 'em," said Joe. "Guarantee you Saint Darrell's gonna drown 'em. Too much character. I don't care who they got. Joe Don Looney. Jimmy Jack Drunk. Anybody. They don't have Scott Appleton. They don't have Tommy Nobis or Mr. Duke Carlisle," he said, referring to Texas's finest players: Appleton, the brilliant tackle; Nobis, the tough, dedicated linebacker; and Carlisle, the resourceful quarterback who preferred to run rather than pass.

Mary Sue and Pat opened the beer, and Joe and

Cecil sang a parody on a hillbilly tune: "I don't care 'bout my gas and oil,/Long as I got my Dare-e-ull Royal,/Mounted on the dashboard o' my car."

They sang it several dozen times until the Cotton Bowl traffic slowed Cecil to a creep along Grand Avenue, one of the main entrance streets. "Joe, baby," Cecil said, "we're gonna have to sell the car, 'cause we got no place to park it."

"Keep goin'. We're gonna get in a lot right up here."

"No chance," said Cecil, observing maybe five thousand parked cars.

"Go on," Joe said. "I'm gonna show you how to ease right on in. Keep goin'. Keep goin'."

Joe said. "Right there! That lot right on the corner, just across from the main entrance. Right there, Cecil, where it says, 'Full House.'"

Cecil turned in amid the frenzied waving and shouting of parking-lot attendants, but Joe leaned out of the window and hollered, "I got a five and a cold beer, podna, if you'll let us in."

Parking was no problem.

The Texas State Fairgrounds on the day of the Oklahoma game are no more crowded than the recreation deck of any ordinary troopship. The ground seems to sag from the weight of hundreds having picnics. "Fried chicken, boys," said Joe, push-

ing along a walkway and observing the people
sprawled on the lawn. "Two necks and a back and a
piece of cold bread."

"And some black French fries," added Cecil. "Best
meal they ever had. Boy, it's fun."

They stopped and bought six beers, two extra, and
finally the voice of Hank Thompson greeted them as
they came near Big Tex, the giant cowboy statue
that is emblematic of the fair and would make fine
kindling wood. Hank Thompson was singing a familiar hillbilly ballad that went, "We got time for one
more drink and a . . . six-pack to go." Joe and Cecil
whooped.

By prearrangement, the Coffmans and Morgans
had planned to meet Joe's sister, Shirley, and his
brother-in-law, David Alter, to straighten out the
ticket situation. Joe had decided that Mary Sue and
Shirley would sit in the end zone while he and David
would take the two seats on the 50-yard line. Joe
thought that seemed fair enough, and no back talk.
Cecil and Pat had their own tickets. The Alters
arrived, and Joe acknowledged them with, "Too
much character, boys. We got too much character to
lose that game." Several beers and Hank Thompson
songs later, they were moving into the Cotton Bowl,
again singing, "I don't care 'bout my gas and oil,/

Long as I got my Dare-e-ull Royal,/Mounted on the dashboard o' my car."

The Texas-Oklahoma game is one of the maddest spectacles of sport. This was the eighteenth consecutive sellout of the series, with 75,504 seats of the stadium crammed with the throatiest, most enthusiastic partisans in football, evenly divided between Texans and Oklahomans. Regardless of the team records, the excitement is there each year; the game matches state against state, school against school, fraternity against fraternity, oil derrick against oil derrick. Some rooters become so emotional that they can see only black on the other side of the field. One who did this year was fullback Harold Philipp of Texas. Before the game, talking about the Texas boys playing on the Oklahoma team, he said: "Why that's just like somebody from the United States playing for Nazi Germany." During the game an immense roar wafts up from the stadium on every play, and the two large bands play "Boomer Sooner," the Oklahoma fight song, and "Texas Fight," the Longhorns' song, an innumerable number of times, always to the accompaniment of a cheering, jeering mob of singers. Occasionally fights break out in the stands.

The game did not provide any opportunities for Joe Coffman to fight, or even to officiate or complain.

Texas was better than even he had expected, and simply swept Oklahoma away, winning 28–7. Joe still managed several excuses for leaping cries of, "Hook 'em Horns," but mainly he occupied himself with pointing out to David Alter some of the more subtle, polished tactics of Darrell Royal's second- and third-teamers. Every time Oklahoma's Jim Grisham, a superb fullback from Olney, Texas, carried the ball, Joe hollered, "Get that turncoat!" And when an OU fan near him would yell encouragement to the Sooners, Joe would quietly remark to his brother-in-law, "Jimmy Jack Drunk back there thinks he's still got a chance to win."

Later, in the usual postgame playing of "The Eyes of Texas" by the Longhorn band down on the field, Joe stood silently proud, pleased and even touched that his team had been so great on the big day. "That song chokes me up every time," he said, forcing a grin. "Man, Dare-e-ull had 'em hot today. You know what Joe Don Looney got? Mr. Scott Appleton gave him zip. Shut him out."

Joyful cries of "Hook 'em Horns" were billowing out of the apartment in north Dallas, the good side of town, or rather, the only side, when the Coffmans, Morgans and Alters got there. Unlike the party the night before, this one was strictly for Longhorns.

Platters of ham and turkey were laid out on a table. A bartender in the kitchen was mixing drinks and opening beers as fast as possible. Wives and girl friends congregated on the sofas. The men pushed into the kitchen and spilled out onto a balcony, drinks lifted, in a continuous toast to Dare-e-ull Royal and Scott Appleton and Duke Carlisle and Tommy Ford and to the memory of college days at Austin. "Hey, Cecil," called Joe. "Just got the score. Florida beat Alabama!"

Cecil slumped back in a chair, laughed heartily, and said, "All I know is, Texas is number one, two, three and four."

After a while, Mary Sue quietly asked Joe if, in the light of the Texas victory, he still intended to drive to Waco for the Baylor-Arkansas game.

"They're still playin', aren't they?" said Joe.

"Well, we'd better do something about dinner," said Mary Sue.

"Get after that turkey and ham," Joe nodded. "Tell you what. Make up some sandwiches and grab six or eight beers out of the icebox and we're gone."

Waco, Texas is noted for only two things. One is that it is the home of Baylor University. The other is that Waco, from time to time, has tornadoes. From Dallas it is about one hour and twenty minutes across the flat north central Texas farmland and, since the Baylor-Arkansas game was mercifully scheduled for 8:00 P.M., the Coffmans and Morgans should have had plenty of time to make the kickoff. But they overstayed the Texas celebration party, and Cecil was moving along too briskly on Highway 77 when the flashing red spotlight on a Texas highway patrol car encouraged him to pull over.

"It's the fuzz," Joe said. "No bad mouth now, Cecil. Don't give him any lip. Just 'Yes sir, Officer, don't hit me no more,' or he'll take us to the Waxahachie jail and nobody'll ever hear from us again."

Cecil Morgan put up a strong argument, but the patrolman decided that he probably ought to have a speeding ticket for $20.50, payable by mail. Cecil had, after all, been driving seventy-five mph in a fifty-five-mph zone.

Joe Coffman writhed in the backseat.

"Don't mind the money, just hate to miss the kickoff," he said.

They missed the whole first quarter, as it turned out. It was just as well. Although Baylor's passing wizard, Don Trull, and its excellent receiver, Lawrence Elkins, staged a wonderful exhibition, the Coffmans and Morgans could not have cared less. They were rooting for Baylor to upset the Razorbacks, which it did 14–10, but the Texas-OU game had drained them of all enthusiasm. "I'd feel okay," said Joe, "if I didn't have dust in my hair, dirt in my nose and sores in my mouth."

The group laughed faintly. Mary Sue and Pat yawned as Don Trull completed a fifty-three-yard pass to Elkins that brought 40,000 other people to their feet. Cecil and Joe pondered quietly the ability of Arkansas to defeat Texas. "No way," Joe decided, sleepily.

"Baylor's sure a swell place." Cecil said, sarcastically. "I saw one of their biggest and oldest fans a while ago, and he's sitting on the goal line. Can you imagine that? No wonder they can't win a championship."

They all yawned again, and soon the game ended. Cecil said he "might could manage" to drive home. Joe said he would pay a hundred dollars if Baylor would let him sleep all night in the parking lot.

"Shame to be this close to Austin and not go," Joe said. "Cecil, what would you give for some crispy, chewy tacos at El Rancho right now? You think El Rancho's chili con queso sounds good? Good Lord!"

The ritual of a football fan, the *real* football fan, in Dallas on Sunday was to attend the Cowboy Club, both before and after the NFL games in the Cotton Bowl. Texas being a dry state (many blame the Baptists and some Texans therefore blame Baylor), the owners of the Cowboys long ago took the precaution of seeing to it that their loyal fans (those who buy memberships) can get a "mixed" drink and something to eat at the club on the state fairgrounds. During the fair and the big football weekend, however, so many people were in town that the club had to move from air-conditioned indoor quarters to a tent just outside of the Cotton Bowl. It was still the place to be on a lazy Sunday that dawned as clear and warm and calm as Friday and Saturday had been. The Cowboys had not won a game and had lost four, but Joe Coffman kept telling people that they were a cinch to beat the Lions. "It's a sure thing," he said to Bedford Wynne, part owner, along with Clint Murchison, Jr., of the Cowboys. "It's an upset weekend, boys. It just figures."

"Hell, I'm startin' to get nervous, now that you told me that," said Bedford.

When a college game has been played in Dallas the day before, the Cowboy Club serves another purpose. It is sort of a hangover haven. Bloody Marys or Bull Shots outsell any other drink, 20–1, and frequently spectators bring their own Bloody Marys in giant thermoses. Since Bedford Wynne, like Joe and Cecil, was one of the most ardent Texas fans in captivity, the Cowboy Club was also a haven for University of Texas fans.

From table to table, the talk was all about the "Horns and that terrific thing they did to Oklahoma Saturday." Mary Sue and Pat sat with a long table of women, discussing the other women across the tent, Joe and Cecil stood, table-hopped, drank, laughed and finally ate two barbecue sandwiches.

"You think the eyeballing ain't something in this place," said Joe, looking around at the women, who even though going to the game, were dressed as fashionably as if they had just stepped out of Nie-man-Marcus. "Got to be headquarters for world champion pretty," he said. "Can't wait for the game to be over so we can come back."

As Joe Coffman had said, it was the Cowboys' day to win. The game lulled along for three quarters, but finally exploded into an offensive spectacular in the fourth quarter, with the Cowboys winning a close one, 17–14.

The crowd was sparse. "Had to be a guts-up fan to make this one on top of all the others," said Joe moodily. "I got to think the crowd's bigger in the Cowboy Club — if they're still serving booze."

Mostly at the insistence of the wives, Mary Sue and Pat, there was yet to be one more stop for them all before the weekend would stagger to a halt. Mary Sue and Pat noted, without an excess of enthusiasm, that they had not eaten a hot meal in two days. The

Beefeater Inn would be nice, said Mary Sue, and it was seldom crowded on a Sunday evening.

"Got to have it," Joe said pleasantly. "Steak, asparagus, coffee and cognac. Got to have it right now." They were there in twenty minutes.

It was a quiet evening, spent mostly in reflection on the four games, and all the people they had seen and in forgetting how much each had drunk. "Guarantee you," Joe said, "we saw everybody but Nasty Jack Kilpatrick."

"Who?" Pat Morgan asked.

"Nasty Jack Kilpatrick," Coffman laughed. "Toughest man I ever knew. Hitchhiked all the way from Miami to Austin one time with nothing but an old toothbrush and a Johnnie Ray record of 'Cry.' Think he wasn't tough?"

In the fatigued after-dinner silence Mary Sue thought it would be a good idea if Joe called Fort Worth long distance to check up on the children.

"Why don't you call, Honey?" Joe asked.

"Please call, Joe," she said.

"Go on, Honey," said Joe.

"You can do it quicker, Joe," Mary Sue said, pleadingly.

Joe Coffman frowned, shoved himself away from the cognac and coffee with a groan.

Walking off, he turned and said, "I'll tell you one

thing, Mary Sue. You just lost yourself a fistful of dimes." A little less than two hours later, tired but full, aching but pleased, oversmoked, overlaughed, dusty-weary but all-victorious, they were home. All four teams had won, all four people had survived.

"Don't forget," said Joe, as he left Cecil and Pat, "we got to get away from here early Friday."

Pat said, "Are we really going to Little Rock for Texas-Arkansas?"

Joe Coffman looked offended.

"They're playin', aren't they?"

# 5

## That Legend Was Loose Again

*The Era of Ara under the giant golden skullcap.*

THE campus was imposing enough just lying there, all leafy and self-haunting. The dome poked into the Indiana sunlight like a giant golden skullcap, the black robes moved quietly through the rust and amber of the trees, and the whole scene hit you with a great, intolerant splat of tradition, mystery and nostalgia. But Notre Dame had always done this, ever since Knute Rockne told his hired help to run that ball, pass that ball, kick that ball and fight-fight-fight-fight, his speeches marking either the end or the beginning of pep talks. Now give the Fighting Irish another powerful football team, and one with something extra special — the Baby Bombers. Why, you didn't have a chance. The most accusing, cynical irreverent infidel among us would have been choked into submission by what Notre Dame is and what Notre Dame was. So there lay me, another simple, limpid captive, whistling the "Victory March" as I struggled up to write.

Even the jokes didn't help very much. I asked if the Gipper ever had a *last* name, by the way, or if the Four Horsemen had cut a new folk album lately. Why did the university swipe its fight song from Webster High in Oklahoma City? How many students were trapped in the underground steam tunnels trying to escape for dates? I asked if the school developed that synthetic rubber only because it might produce better shoulder pads, if it founded the first germ-free laboratory in order to manufacture halfbacks who wouldn't fumble, if the Sacred Heart Church was where everyone went to seek forgiveness for beating Purdue only 26–14, if it really took graduates three years to get married because girls figured it would be at least that long before they recovered from the pep rallies. And I asked if a perfect 10–0 season would be what Father Hesburgh ordered when he said his goal was "the attainment of excellence."

Notre Dame only retaliated with a humor of its own, a humor it could well afford now that it again had an instant legend in the passing combination of Terry Hanratty to Jim Seymour. It was a natural humor the campus derived from a football past that included thirteen national championships, nineteen undefeated teams, twenty-three teams with only one loss, eighteen teams with only two losses, one hundred and ten All-America selections, six Heisman Trophy winners and just six losing seasons out of seventy-seven.

Someone in South Bend, Ind. would show you the statue of Father Corby outside a priests' residence near Sorin Hall, the aging bronze mold of a man holding up his right arm ("There's old fair-catch Corby"). Someone would point to a more modern chunk of metal near the library — Moses, an arm uplifted, forefinger gesturing to the heavens ("We're number one"). Someone would show you another figure, this one in the huge mosaic on the library — Christ raising both arms ("Six points"). Someone would point to a deserted patch of grass adjacent to the big brick stadium. Vacant now, it was where old Cartier Field stood, the rickety wooden plant of 20,000 capacity in which Rockne's teams played. In the early 1960's it got one last historical footnote. While the new library was being built, excavation work resulted in a large mound of dirt on Cartier Field, on the ground where George Gipp (some say Ronald Reagan) had trod. The students gave it a fitting name: Mount Excellence.

Finally you would be led to the Old Council Oak

in a shady cemetery near the campus. There, beneath the ground where La Salle once sat smoking a peace pipe with the Indians, rest the bones of Knute Rockne, who, as every self-respecting football fan knows, died in a plane crash at forty-three, having given the sport most of the glamour it thrives on today. There is, of course, nothing funny about Rockne's death, but inasmuch as the grave site had been visited in recent years mostly by out-of-town newspapermen it had become known to some as the Department of Journalism. Rockne would love it.

So Notre Dame could outjoke you, too. It could even joke about its two rampaging sophomores, quarterback Hanratty and end Seymour, who were so stupendous, so fantastic, at midseason that they had the Fighting Irish up there again, the echoes awakened, the thunder shaking down from the sky and all of the loyal sons marching, marching, out of their insurance offices, accounting firms and good, solid suburban-citizen obscurity with a pride that never really had to be resurrected — only controlled.

It happened so quickly. The first time Hanratty drew back and sidearmed the football roughly fifty miles in the air and Seymour caught it without breaking his long-gaited stride, a natty, subtle little fellow who resided in a cellar office on the Notre Dame campus knew he would be in dire need of a suitable nickname for the combination. Roger Valdi-serri was the sports publicity man in South Bend, and he was a good one. When he replaced old-timer Charlie Callahan, he had said, "They finally got an Irishman." Roger had been a lifelong sideliner at the school. He was once secretary to boy coach Terry Brennan and he still did one of the superior Frank Leahy imitations.

After that first game Roger went right to work.

"Without Grantland Rice, we might be in trouble," he said. "I've already read a Dynamic Duo some-where."

"Well, it doesn't have quite the ring of the Bard of Staten Island," I said.

"What about the Touchdown Tikes?" he said.

"It's not the Springfield Rifle."

"Yeah. Bertelli," Roger said.

Then he said, "What about — it's just a chance, of course — but what about the Diaper Demons? No? The Terrifying Twins? No. Uh, the Terrible Two. No, no. Uh, the, uh, the Torrid Twosome. Well . . .

"You know what these kids are gonna do?" he continued.

"They're so much on fire with the press and all? These two kids are so good they're gonna knock me out of six All-Americas, and if they're that good they deserve a catchy nickname."

"Six All-Americas? *Six* besides Hanratty and Seymour?"

Roger said, "Well, you figure Nick Eddy at halfback for sure, and Jim Lynch at linebacker. If anybody picks an authentic fullback, it has to be Larry Conjar. You'd think Tom Regner for an offensive guard. He's just the best there is. Then our two defensive tackles, Pete Duranko and Kevin Hardy. Big, strong, quick — the pros love 'em. You think maybe you could land them on something. Now, though, with these two kids on fire . . ."

He signed and said, "It's awfully scary. Do you know that in his first four games Hanratty threw for more yards than George Gipp, Harry Stuhldreher, Marchy Schwartz, Bill Shakespeare, Johnny Lujack, Frank Tripucka and Daryle Lamonica did in their best seasons? Do you realize that in his first *two* games Seymour caught *more* passes for *more* yardage than Leon Hart did the year he won the Heisman Trophy?"

Roger Valdiserri sighed. None of the new names seemed any better than the Baby Bombers, his original thought, which was not bad, considering that Granny, Damon, Ring, Westbrook, Heywood and all the gang managed to use up practically everything else palatable long before Roger's time and duty. The Baby Bombers would stick.

Meanwhile Notre Dame's success resounded across the country, where there were 178 alumni clubs and a thousand more fugitive groups, the sub-way-prairie-mountain-swamp alumni who knew nothing of the university's excellent academic role. They were oblivious to its high standards in science and liberal arts, to its notable research in economics and aeronautics — even to the strict disciplinary customs that made it a kind of Catholic semimilitary institution without uniforms. They certainly did not know it as a school curiously capable of turning out such a cross section of men as Dr. Tom Dooley; Edwin O'Connor, the bestselling novelist; Walt Kennedy, commissioner of the National Basketball Association; Bill Miller, the former New York Congressman who was Barry Goldwater's vice-presidential running mate; Jack Schneider, the "third man from the top" at CBS; and Red Smith, America's best-known sports columnist.

Notre Dame fans feast on all of their lore, good or bad, and part of the fun that Hanratty and Seymour were creating came from relishing all of the old tales about all of the people who came before coach Ara Parseghian and his Baby Bombers. There had been several box formations of them, but for Notre Dame insiders, whether they spewed forth the memories in bars or restaurants, in homes or offices, the person who dominated their conversations was Frank Leahy, the man who really drew open the curtains for the Era of Ara.

Though he won five national titles in eleven seasons, Frank Leahy was everything Notre Dame loved and disliked at the same time. He was loved, of course, because he won games, but he also was frequently criticized for some of the ways that his teams won. There was the sucker shift, for instance, and the feigned injury. There were charges of dirty play and illegal recruiting. There were accusations of unethical practice sessions. But through it all Leahy outwardly remained a theatrically charming personality, a grim strategist and, best of all, a winner. He would spend many a night in a room in the campus firehall, thirty miles from his home in Michigan City, Indiana, worrying about a team the oddsmakers knew he would devour by forty points. He would attempt pep talks with tears and brooding, with sadness and hatred, and always, as one former player said, "in his high-pitched Boston College speech-course Irish."

When Leahy talked, some players, like Johnny Lujack, listened intently, as if the loss of a single syllable might result in a tragic interception. Others didn't. Terry Brennan had a tendency to nap; he knew he would play his best, and few played better.

Ziggy Czarobski frequently seized the occasion to go to the bathroom. Given enough time, Czarobski might have driven Leahy nutty. Or nuttier. After one particularly disappointing Saturday — the Irish had won by only three touchdowns, or something — Leahy announced that the team was going to learn the game all over again. From the primer. "Oh, lads," he said. "We'll start from here. I hold in my hand a leather ball inflated with air. Now, who can tell me what this is?"

Czarobski said, "Hey, Coach, not so fast."

In moments of frustration and rare excitement, Leahy was known to treat his players with unwarranted scorn, although he would forgive them later on. When Jim Shrader missed an extra point in the Pittsburgh game of 1952, a point that would have tied the score, the coach lunged at him on the sideline, grabbed him by the shoulders and yelled, "Oh, Jim Shrader, you'll burn in hell for this!"

Despite his fierce competitive nature, his agonizing lectures and self-torturing worry, Leahy had a sense of humor that bubbled up on odd occasions. In a September workout before the season of 1953, his last before retirement, Leahy decided he would conclude the drills by rehearsing his injury play — a play, incidentally, that later enabled Notre Dame to tie Iowa and remain unbeaten.

"Oh, lads," he said. "Let us practice the injury play." Frank Varrichione, the tackle, knew what to do. He was the designated victim, so after the usual collision of bodies, Varrichione clutched at his leg, moaned, whimpered, hollered and flip-flopped around like a man who had truly been wounded. Out onto the field raced Leahy.

"Frank," he said. "I think we'd better make it total unconsciousness."

And all of the rest of those stories.

They lead to Ara Parseghian, restorer of the glory that was, janitor of the debris left by the unfortunate Brennan's five years during obvious de-emphasis and Joe Kuharich's four unspectacular seasons, during which George Izo, a good passer, injured his leg while miscast as a defensive back. Although everything Ara added up to still seemed wrong for Notre Dame — a Protestant and a graduate of another school (Miami of Ohio) — everything he was and said and did was perfect. Everything.

For one thing, Ara Parseghian was a brilliant offensive coach, as he had proved at Northwestern. He beat teams he should not have beaten, and with fewer athletes. For another thing, Ara Parseghian was smart enough to know you must have a loyal, hard-working staff and, in his particular case, a defensive specialist. He had such a staff, and it featured defensive coach John Ray, who had set six NCAA defensive records at John Carroll in 1962.

Like Parseghian himself, John Ray was a fiery, persuasive, resonant man who, from the beginning in the near-perfect year of 1964, had constructed a distinctive spirit in the defensive unit equal to that in Ara's spicy offensive platoons. Though Ray disliked seeing it put quite this way, Notre Dame had, in effect, two head coaches, one for offense and one for defense, both of them highly accomplished, as the record indicated. "It's Ara's team," John Ray argued, honestly. But Ara countered with equal kindness. "John deserves full credit for our defense," he said.

The casual fan did not realize it, but a lot of head coaches did not treat their assistants with the concern, tact and understanding that Parseghian did. Some had rules that the assistant may not speak to the press, may not be seen in highlight films, may not appear at clinics, address luncheons or attend conventions. This type of head coach was invariably a loser, though it is not implied that there aren't other ways to be one. Ara Parseghian was a winner, and he was as generous with his assistants as possible.

But the surface of the man was what Notre Dame followers liked the best, the things they could see and hear. Take Ara at a Friday night pregame rally in the gymnasium, which was as close as free men

could come to a prison riot for better food and
bedding. Or Ara leaping around on the sidelines
during a game, hugging players, shouting instructions and encouragement. Or Ara at the end of a
day's practice, building his squad lecture to a cre-
scendo, combining, one is told, the passion of Rockne
with the dedication of Leahy.

For all of this intensity, the Irish workouts would
be fun and certainly not agony sessions. Every successful team goes about things differently, so you
can't say whether Parseghian's procedures were the
best. But there was more chatter, more hustling,
more continuously earnest activity on the part of
everybody than at a great variety of other campuses.

Maybe the Notre Dame coaches simply had louder
voices. You didn't have to be all the way down on the
end of the field with the defense to hear blond and
husky John Ray, for example.

"Where were *you?*" he shouted to a player who
had missed an assignment. "Were you *here,* like a
good, smart Notre Dame man? Or were you *there?*
Come on, come on, come on. Let me see the defense
the way *Notre Dame* plays it."

And up on Ara Parseghian's end of the grass the
Baby Bombers were at work. Over and over again,
Terry Hanratty slung the bomb and Seymour got
there. A flat pass, a screen, a hook, then the deep one

again — and Seymour had it. The ball didn't seem to touch the ground for an interminable number of plays.

Notre Dame had seen a lot of passing combinations through the years: George Gipp to Eddie Anderson, Harry Stuhldreher to Don Miller, Angelo Bertelli to John Yonakor, Lujack to Brennan, Bob Williams to Leon Hart and then to Jim Mutscheller, Ralph Guglielmi to Joe Heap, Paul Hornung to Jim Morse, and Johnny Huarte to Jack Snow. Forget them. Nobody ever threw a football to anybody until the Baby Bombers found each other.

Notre Dame knew it. Off to the side, Tom Pagna, the assistant coach in charge of the offensive backfield, hid his delight in a joke.

"Just think," Pagne said. "When Terry came to me, he was all knuckles."

Presently the drills were over, and the offensive and defensive squads thundered to the middle of the field, still clattering, whooping, laughing. Suddenly the defense gathered around John Ray and began an ancient football chant.

"Two bits, four bits, six bits, a dollar," they yelled and you thought instantly, hold it, John it's corny, it's —

"All for the *offense*, stand up and holler."

Silence. Hilarious silence.

Now the offense began to appreciate the joke, as laughter all around intruded, and Ray walked away to bum a cigarette, leaving the squad to Ara Parseghian.

No one could hear what Ara said at first. It had something to do with why Notre Dame won, you assumed. But his voice was rising. You could hear him now. Louder. Still louder. Yeeek, he was shouting. "Are they gonna score on us?" he exploded. "Are they gonna do to us what they did last year?" Even louder. Rockne. Leahy. "Are we gonna score on *them?* Are we? Are we gonna beat 'em? Are we gonna beat the *hell* out of 'em?"

Yeah, yeah, yeah, yeah, yeah, and Ara strolled calmly away, eating a mint, another day's work done.

"Hey," said the coach, smiling, reaching out to shake hands. "Boy, we got bad luck for sure with you here. I saw you a while ago, standing over there on the other side of the field so you'd have to look into the sun. That's how smart writers are." He grinned at John Ray.

"Well, they're all here, or coming," said Ara. "In mid-season, just like sixty-four. Newspapers, magazines, television, radio — the whole works." He looked away, momentarily wistful. "It's great to get publicity and all that, but I wish, like every other coach, that it could all come *after* the season, when these young kids have done it — *if* they do it."

Ara consoled himself. "Well, they're great kids. They're handling it real good. That's the thing — they're such great kids. But, geez, the stuff going on. Everybody wants 'em to pose for a magazine cover, everybody wants a private interview. I'm tripping over television cable right here on my own practice field!

"Hey," Ara continued. "That goofy Klosterman called the other day." The reference was to Don Klosterman, then the general manager of the Houston Oilers. "He wanted to know if Roger couldn't rig up a morals charge on Seymour so he could sign him."

"A lot of the pros think Seymour could start for them right now."

Ara said, "Well, he's a good one, all right. We knew he was good. We knew Hanratty was good, too. But we were afraid to think *how* good. I'll tell you, I still don't know how good they are. Hanratty doesn't throw a perfect ball, by any means. He's strong, as you've seen. But he throws a hard, tight spiral, a heavier ball than most passers. It's a ball that most receivers think is hard to catch. He has a tendency to throw too low. We're working hard on him to come up here with it. The best thing he has is strength and accuracy on the long ones. You can teach a kid to throw short, as they say. But you can't teach him to throw long if he hasn't got the arm."

Ara went on. "You can stop that, though. You don't have to let us hit the long one. In football you can stop anything you want to stop, but you have to give up something else. North Carolina wanted to stop Seymour. They doubled and tripled him. So we ran. Eddy and Conjar saw it open up for them. The one time North Carolina singled Jimmy, we had the right play called. And that's when Terry hit him for fifty-six yards."

So it had all worked beautifully. Hanratty had completed 51 passes for 972 yards and five touchdowns, and Seymour had caught 34 of them for 675 yards and five touchdowns, and when the defenses had chosen to concentrate on the Baby Bombers the running game had knifed out 1,229 yards. Even when the two sophomores hadn't been trying to connect, their mere presence had worried their opponents into shock. They would continue doing it until another national title was part of South Bend lore.

But who were they, anyway, these two teenagers who had pumped so much unexpected drama and excitement into the 1966 collegiate season? Basically they were just a couple of kids who had nothing more startling to reveal in their characters than politeness and wonderment, and nothing more dome-shaking to say than, "No, sir, I sure didn't expect anything like this to happen."

The receiving end of this pass-and-catch sensation, Jim Seymour, came from Berkley, Michigan. There were enough Seymours to choose up for a game of backyard touch — four brothers and one sister besides Jim, one of whom, John, played halfback at Army for three years. Fortunately, the father, Bart, was well off, the vice-president of a company called Imperial Metallic Lubricants, Inc., a Detroit firm that sold oil products to industry. Bart appeared to have sold a lot. The Seymour home was large, elegantly furnished and had a swimming pool.

Jim Seymour was so impressive an athlete that simply stating what he was and what he could do came out almost like lies. Take the size and speed. He was 6 feet 4 and weighed 208 pounds and ran the hurdles. Now, really. Then you put him at his position, end, and you give him an acrobat's moves and leg spring and, quite frankly, the damnedest pair of hands any pro scout had ever seen on a sophomore, and what you had was instant touchdown, the perfect receiver for Hanratty.

Seymour had proved that he could run all the

patterns Ara charted and that he was exceptionally dangerous on the long ones, where his smooth, powerful speed left a defensive man alone and embarrassed. But then, while he was in open throttle, looking like a 440 man on the backstretch, here came the ball from Hanratty, and Jim simply sort of brought it in — a man taking a can of peas off a shelf. He had done it at least once against every team he had met, and twice or three times against most. In the Purdue game alone he pulled down 13 for 276 yards and three touchdowns.

"I was so frightened in that opening game," Jim's mother said. "I was afraid he would look bad. And after he caught the first two, I said, 'Sit down, that's enough.' Shows you how good a judge I am."

The pro scouts were the best judges, and Seymour already had driven many of them out of their usual nonchalance, not to mention their rented cars.

"I'll tell you what," one of them said. "There has never been a kid at his position who has his size, his speed, his move, his hands and his attitude. He's got to be the most unreal thing that's ever come along. I can't think of a pro club he couldn't start for right now. The only guy who remotely resembles him in the pros is Boyd Dowler. And he's pretty good, isn't he? You know what? I'd take Seymour."

At such praise, the Notre Dame split end was

mystified and aghast, although I noted that he could wrap a neat four-in-hand knot in his tie, centered, without the aid of a mirror. He had also taught himself to play the guitar and cook almost any dish he wanted to eat. There were a lot of people who might rank these talents up there with catching touchdown passes.

"I've dropped too many for everyone to get so excited," Jim said, smiling easily. He was handsome and personable in a Roger Staubach kind of way — scrubbed, wide grin, white teeth, neatly dressed. "There are a lot of things I've got to learn. I haven't even begun to see any variety of defenses yet. And I think I have trouble catching the low passes. I'm working on that."

Seymour's partner, Terry Hanratty, was half Irish and half Italian, a condition that had encouraged Roger Valdiserri, naturally, to tell Parseghian that the quarterback's last name ought to be spelled with an "i." Hanratty came from an entirely different background than Seymour — a separated family in Butler, Pa. His mother had not yet seen him play, except against Purdue on television, but it was not because she always hoped that he would become a baseball player. "I pushed him in sports all my life," she said. "I wanted him to play baseball, but I always told him, if you want something out of life, you can get it through sports."

Hanratty's father, Eddie, was a sports-loving man himself, who once considered a boxing career. He won sixteen or seventeen bouts as an amateur, but gave it up because, as he said, "You can wind up on Goofy Street." The father had seen three Notre Dame games, sitting proudly but worriedly in the stands, fearing injury. "He'll see a lot of mountains of men before he's through," said the father, "and I'll have to try to act like I'm not worried about it."

The quarterback was not easily recruited by Notre Dame. His first choice was Penn State, and his second was Michigan State, even though he had an older brother, Pete, who had gone to South Bend on a part-scholarship for track and field. Penn State said that Hanratty's grades didn't measure up, but Notre Dame said that John Ray, also a top recruiter, was the final persuading factor. Hanratty confessed the same.

Terry Hanratty was polite, bewildered, mannerly. He said, "I've just been trying to beat out Coley O'Brien for quarterback, and now all this happens." But that's not all he said. After the spectacular day against Purdue when he completed 16 passes for 304 yards and three touchdowns, Hanratty was named

Midwest Back of the Week — not the biggest deal in the world. But Hanratty was called into Valdiserri's office and told of the honor, nonetheless. The quarterback, who had sharp features in a narrow face and a black crew cut that lay flat, looked stunned. After a pause, he said slowly, "Boy, I never thought it would all end up like this."

Terry was like that. So was Jim Seymour. And before the two of them got through, Notre Dame almost had to erect a couple more statues.

# 6

## Vamp to Daylight

*Halfback Shirley MacLaine and the worst Notre Dame team ever assembled.*

**E**XPERIENCED moviegoers always know what to expect when Hollywood tries to get serious with the subject of football. In the stark, brutal, devastating opening scene, coach Goldie Nails, who is tough as nails but has a heart of gold, prepares for State's big game against Normal by sweeping through a tap-dance routine in the campus malt shop. Everything is uphill after that. Goldie staggers out of his tap dance to make a woeful discovery. His star fullback, Crew Slammer, has been caught cheating on an exam. Goldie, of course, discovers that the big, rugged, good-natured Crew has been framed and that the person who framed him — since Hollywood has always been harsh on intellectuals in football movies — is the scrawny, squeak-voiced bookworm, Fitzhugh Clarence, who is jealous over the affections of (choose one) Bonita Granville, Ann Rutherford or Priscilla Lane. Fitzhugh is soon tortured into a confession by a group of teasing coeds who play keep away with his skullcap. But it is too late. Crew Slammer, having grown despondent, has disappeared: gone back to log-rolling country. The burden of beating Normal thus falls directly onto the shoulders of the cocky sophomore, Brick Thompson, a triple threat who can run, pass and sing. The trouble with Brick is that he has been kidnapped by gamblers. Happily, however, all ends well for State. With a minute to play and the score tied, Brick Thompson suddenly appears on the field, having escaped from the clutches of Sheldon Leonard and Elisha Cook Jr., squats down, says "hup," takes the snap and, amid some mysterious film clips of Elroy (Crazylegs) Hirsch dashing through the San Francisco '49ers, wins the game, the girl and the last production number.

Hollywood has made this movie a lot of times, in varying forms, and called it *Saturday's Hero, College Coach, The College Widow, Pigskin Parade, One Minute to Play, The Forward Pass, The Big Game, The Drop Kick, The All American, Brown of Harvard, Spirit of West Point, Harmon of Michigan, The Spirit of Stanford, Touchdown Army! Crazylegs,*

*Knute Rockne — All American* and several other big, rugged, good-natured things. Rarely has the film intended to be humorous, but just as rarely has it ever been anything else.

The best thing about Hollywood football movies is that with precious little aging they soon become classics of whimsy and satire on late-evening television. And maybe it is precisely because of this unwanted success that the formula never seems to change. But there was this time, nevertheless, that some Hollywood types got together with the very novel idea of trying to make a football movie that was *supposed* to be funny. It would try to prove nothing more realistic than the fact that Shirley MacLaine was as cute in gridiron gear as she was in a harem costume and, in any case, that she was a loon.

Unfortunately, when the movie was finished it didn't prove much beyond this, except that the old films are funnier still, and nowhere near as cornball even if Jack Oakie and Frank McHugh stand up and sing the Minnesota Rowser. As a starter, it bore the insane title of *John Goldfarb, Please Come Home!* and was about Notre Dame. It had Shirley MacLaine as a cheerleader who scored a winning touchdown in a game played in the desert. It had a cast that included Peter Ustinov as an Arab king who drove a golf

cart, Richard Crenna as a lost U-2 pilot named John
Goldfarb, Scott Brady as the Notre Dame coach, and
ten camels, eight harem wives, fifty tribesmen, four
football officials, twenty sheiks, thirty-six Bedouin
warriors, a black bear, four Nubian slaves, sixteen
musicians, seven Tangier dancers, eight cheerleaders, twenty-two Arabian football players, twenty-
two Notre Dame football players, four camel riders
and a monkey.

The parties responsible for bringing about this
unlikely assembly were coproducers Steve Parker,
who was married to Shirley MacLaine, and J. Lee
Thompson, who had directed Shirley MacLaine, and
screen writer William Peter Blatty, who wrote for
Shirley MacLaine. The plot that brought them all together, along with the camels, harem girls and Notre
Dame players, was — as one might have suspected —
not very firmly grounded in South Bend history.
Briefly, it dealt with the king of a land called Fawzia
and his efforts to schedule Notre Dame for a postseason game on his own Arabic field against Fawz U.;
with the efforts of a girl reporter from *Strife* magazine
to get a dead-level story on a harem while remaining
upright herself; with the efforts of a bumbling
United States government to see that Notre Dame
both plays and loses (better for foreign relations);

and with the efforts of a U-2 pilot to coach an Arabian football team that believes the best way to bat down a pass is with a rifle.

"The plot," said Blatty, "was basically inspired by Francis Gary Powers." There were a few other considerations. Shirley MacLaine wanted to do a comedy, Shirley MacLaine's husband wanted to produce one, Blatty wanted to write one and 20th Century-Fox wanted to release one. And everyone thought that it might make money. Right?

"They're playing my song," said Blatty, a dark, solemn-faced man. "We were sitting around one night at Steve and Shirley's talking about the Powers thing. I said wouldn't it be a funny movie if you like did something crazy with it. Steve said write it, he'd produce it and Shirley would play it. First, I thought make the guy Jewish and the Arabs get him. Then I'm watching one of those old football movies on TV one night and I thought make him a football coach. Being a fan of the poor L. A. Rams, I think about football a lot anyhow."

As everyone concerned might well have guessed from the start, the making of *Goldfarb* was destined to become an athletic event in itself. The interior scenes were routine enough, with the exception of Notre Dame's pregame meal, which involved harem girls and dancing. Then, for the game sequences, the company moved from the Fox lot to a secluded area in the Mojave Desert called Rosamond Dry Lake. Rosamond is a flat, bleak stretch of sand near Edwards Air Force Base. Twelve miles from Lancaster, California, and ninety miles from Los Angeles, the site was selected because it looked like Fawzia ought to look — a flimsily disguised Saudi Arabia with Peter Ustinov. And it was complete with mirages.

"Who won the regatta today?" Shirley MacLaine asked, after getting her first look at Rosamond Dry Lake. To which Richard Crenna replied, "I don't know. The flamingos obstructed my view."

Even in a football motion picture that is designed to be humorous there must be traces of realism. Therefore Fox spent $12,000 building an actual field in the middle of the desert. Workmen spread two inches of soil over the sand, then laid down six-by-eight-foot strips of Kentucky bluegrass that had been trucked in from a Tehachapi turf farm. To keep the grass alive, the studio brought in more trucks, equipped with sprinkler systems to shower ten thousand gallons of water a day on the playing field. Around the field it erected a grandstand, complete with a king's throne, ornate goalposts, minarets, a

scoreboard straight out of Baghdad, a phony palace
façade propped up with two-by-fours and some
studio palm trees — the only trees anywhere near
Rosamond Dry Lake.

"Those trees," explained studio publicity man Don
Prince, who wore a burnoose and identified himself to
everybody as Florence of Arabia, "are the same ones
we shipped to Hawaii for South Pacific so we could
place them where we wanted them and not have
God's palms dictate our camera angles."

The workmen and special-effects crew had one
more small task to perform before Notre Dame could
meet Hollywood in the Fawz Bowl. The script called
for oil gushers to spout up regularly during the
game. This was accomplished by having pipes laid
underground from a tank to strategic locations
around the handmade field. A black and greasy
liquid would spray forth. The gushers did not look
exactly like Spindletop, but they looked real enough
and made an impressive enough mess when
turned on.

With the set completed and everyone on hand —
stars, extras, technicians — an outsider unused to the
ways of Hollywood might with good reason have
guessed that the subject was not football but war
(which might have been appropriate since Director

Thompson had done *Guns of Navarone* and director of photography Leon Shamroy had done — Fox should excuse the word — *Cleopatra*).

Loosely clustered around the desert were tents, trailers, buses, tractors, trucks, cranes, camera booms, automobiles, jeeps, camels and brigades of bronzed, bemuscled young men.

If a program had been printed listing the starting lineups for the Notre Dames and the Fawzians, it would have been funnier than the movie by far. Notre Dame, for example, fielded a team consisting of Craig Chudy, 6 feet 3, 220, ex-UCLA, ex-Steeler and ex-49er playing at left end; Bruce Underhill, 6 feet 2, 250, ex-UCLA, at left tackle; Kent McWhirter 6 feet 2, 230, ex-Utah, at left guard; Robert West, 6 feet 1, 210, ex-Jones Country Junior College, at center; Jim Martin, 6 feet 2, 238, ex-Notre Dame All-America and ex-Detroit Lion All-Pro, at right guard; Kent Miller, 6 feet 5, 220, ex-UCLA basketball, at right tackle; Glenn Wilder, 6 feet 1, 200, ex-USC, at right end; Jim Dawson, 6 feet 1, 200, ex-UCLA, at quarterback; Ron Brown, 6 feet, 185, ex-USC, at halfback; Jim Steffen, 6 feet, 200, ex-UCLA, current Washington Redskin, at halfback; and Jerry Okuneff, 5 feet 11, 210, ex-UCLA, at fullback.

The Fawz team had individual credentials of a more singular nature. Its lineup read Jack (Ding-a-

ling) Bellin, general contractor, at left end; Sam
(Muffler) Midas, garbage collector, at left tackle;
Ron Dawson, actor, at left guard; Ted Grossman,
policeman and comedian, at center; George Sheffield,
actor, at right guard; Bill (Peanuts) Weiss, former
national weight-lifting champion and stuntman, at
right tackle; Irving Koszewski, former Mr. Universe
runner-up, at right end; Lou Elias, stunt man, at
quarterback; Guy Way, actor, at halfback; Garry
Downey, actor and world traveler, at halfback; and
Dick Sweet, muscleman, extra and freelance karate
practitioner, at fullback.

The man responsible for, or rather guilty of, naming the lineups was Jim Dawson, tackle and captain of
UCLA's 1957 team, who had been talent chief for
the Oakland Raiders and a scout for the Los Angeles
Rams. He was hired for *Goldfarb* as technical ad-
viser. In that capacity he advised about the purchase
of $3,000 worth of authentic Notre Dame uniforms.
And being an ex-lineman, he also advised that he
play in the backfield.

Not even Jim Dawson knew how much technical
advising he was going to have to do, but when
Director Thompson got started shooting the game
scenes where Notre Dame built a 21–16 lead, it became clear that the monkey or the bear knew as
much about football as the director.

One of the first questions Thompson, a Briton who had never seen a game of American football, asked Dawson was, "Jim, exactly in what manner should the umpire toss his hanky?"

The shooting began believably enough with Notre Dame scoring a touchdown on its first play, an end run where people like Jim Martin, Craig Chudy, Jim Steffen and Glenn Wilder caught a lot of Arabs from the blind sides and took some excruciating advantage of them.

"This is really great," said Dawson. "You get to do all kinds of things here that you never got to do enough of in college. Really cream a guy."

Somewhat ghoulishly, Dawson insisted on brief rehearsals between Notre Dame tacklers and Fawzian ballcarriers before a scene was filmed. In one particularly awesome run-through, the entire Notre Dame line got in ready position, someone pitched a ball to an unsuspecting Fawzian — "Like he's getting ready to fair catch a punt," Dawson said in a voice that was gleefully sad — and then the Notre Dame onrushers buried the Fawzians in the Kentucky bluegrass.

As the game sequences continued, the plot got crazier, the players more bewildered and Thompson paid less attention to whatever semblance of football realism there had ever been.

"This is some deal," said Martin, who filled out a uniform the way a harem girl fitted into a costume she could keep in her purse. He was strolling back to the sideline after a take. "Did you see what that silly script had us do? We're on the one-yard line and they had me kick a field goal. Top of that, Thompson lets the Fawzies climb up on their shoulders and block it! Some football."

Another time, Fawz kicked off to Notre Dame, and Thompson promptly gave the ball to Fawz, Dawson objected. He explained the rules. Thompson calmly listened and then said, "Well, that's a horrid rule."

Off to one side, Blatty, the writer, said, "Jim doesn't understand that it'll all come out okay in the editing. Anyhow, maybe the secret to making a movie about football is to have a director who doesn't know a thing about the game. J. Lee does come up with some great ones. What's offsides? What do you mean, a quarter? What does it mean when the king says, 'Win one for the Gipper?' Why is it funny that the Fawz line is known as the Seven Pillars of Wisdom? Things like that."

"It's nutty," said Jim Dawson. "That's show biz, Tootsie," said Blatty.

Thompson, a tiny, lean bundle of energy in enormous dark glasses whose idea of after-work entertainment was to eat five bowls of hot sauce at a

Mexican restaurant, had his own conclusions. "The only thing I've found out for myself around here about football is that a good British rugby team could beat Notre Dame any day," he said. "People say I don't know the game. Of course I know it. Look here. The only real difference between the American game and ours is that you pass the ball forward and we pass it backward. And in that respect our game is much more artistic."

Moviemaking is a painfully tedious business, mainly because directors insist on shooting every scene from every conceivable camera angle. During the long, drowsy pauses in the desert sun the players spilled across the field in shorts to sunbathe, rolled under trailers and sound trucks to sleep or read, sat around crates and boxes to play cards and drink beer, played lazy games of touch football and sometimes, in more energetic moments, romped off across the sand in pursuit of a harem girl.

One afternoon near the completion of the picture, everyone seemed a little perkier than usual. Several busloads of people from Hollywood trade papers, agencies and newspapers roamed the premises. The men, columnists included, removed their shirts, and the women stared hypnotically at the ponderous athletes. A helicopter landed and unloaded Steve

Parker, who had flown in from Tokyo. He took off his shirt. Publicity man Don Prince drove up with a trailer full of beer. A camel groaned. And the stars wandered around like just plain folks.

Scott Brady, a husky Irishman who claimed he was a true Notre Dame fan and a former member of New York's subway alumni, playfully assembled some members of his team and said, "I only got me one rule on this squad. No beer before ten in the morning." And he went for a beer.

Returning, Brady said, 'Know my name in this movie? Clip Sakalakis. You know something else? It's easier to pronounce than Ara Parseghian."

Richard Crenna, who wore Levi's and a white T-shirt that said I WILL NOT on the front, explained that he knew a lot about sports — played golf, rooted for USC, portrayed Daffy Dean in *The Pride of St. Louis.* A dancer named Teri or Lori or Micki or Sandi injected a note of gossip when she said, "Did you hear that Bill Eckhardt (the unit manager) fired the slaves? They wanted to take a shower."

Following the laughter, Crenna said with a twang, "I been afearin' a range war. The sheepmen tore down our fence. It don't look good at all."

Peter Ustinov wore a yellow terry-cloth robe and a large sombrero. He chatted with columnists, drew caricatures of cast members on scratch paper, talked of his favorite sport, tennis, and sports car racing, his second favorite. "I've only seen American football on television," he said. "But I have the feeling it isn't as rugged a sport as rugby. They don't wear so much protective padding in the British Isles. In fact, I believe they've discovered it's one way to hold down the population."

Presently the population on the sidelines was increased by the appearance of a slow-moving, shapely female figure in snug dungarees, coolie hat, yellow silk blouse, sandals, sunglasses and beer can.

As the young woman approached, a prostrate Notre Dame player held up his hand from the grass and said, "May I?"

"May you what?"

"Kiss you, of course," said the player.

"Have you got that much time?" said Shirley MacLaine, gliding past to take up residence in a patch of shade by a trailer.

There, she flopped down and talked with a stand-in, showing as much interest as she did when talking to an important shirtless columnist about a variety of subjects that included Vietnam, football, travel, booze, politics, Mexican food, the ballet and herself.

For one of Hollywood's superstars, Shirley MacLaine seemed to be a refreshing betrayal of the Sunset Boulevard legends. Around her there were no ego builders, pamperers or flunkeys, and she fetched her own beer. She was unashamed to expose herself without makeup, thereby revealing some freckles. "I'm just thankful I'm photogenic," she said, licking her upper lip, which she seemed fond of doing.

Being a star, Shirley did not have to stay in a motel in Lancaster during the last days of *Goldfarb*. The studio would gladly have transported her to and from the desert if she had wanted to stay home in Encino, a suburb of L.A. "Being on time and getting a movie over with is part of being a pro," she said. "Besides, I got other things to do, like travel." Shirley therefore chose to stay in Lancaster at the Desert Inn and to do her relaxing in the motel bar — the Rogue Room — before strangers who may have been startled by her language, which was once described by the *New York Times* as "briny."

Now in the shade of the trailer, preparing for makeup and wardrobe and watching the workmen build a track down the middle of the field for a camera truck, Shirley was just as lively as she was in the Rogue Room in the evenings, where her conversation had taken care of just about every ill known to man, including the Desert Inn's habit of serving orange sherbet on the same plate with steak and onion rings.

"Sure I know a lot about football," she said. "I was

a damn cheerleader in high school (Washington-Lee in Arlington, Virginia) for three years. That was a big deal, too." Licking her lip and considering the crucial scene she was about to do, she smiled. "What a movie. A dumb broad runs through the whole Notre Dame team."

While Shirley disappeared to put on her Fawzian football gear, which consisted of a helmet emblazoned with dancing girls, low-quarter football shoes, shoulder pads and a long red robe, the Notre Dame and Arab players began rehearsing their parts on the field. They threw side body blocks, leg slips and two-on-ones. They did roll-unders. They practiced diving headlong through the air and stumbling in pursuit of a ballcarrier that they dared not bruise.

Soon Thompson, by now recovered from his hot sauce of the night before, announced that he was ready for the big run. At this point choreographer Paul Godkin, wearing a flowered sports shirt, bathing suit and white moccasins, called for all of the harem girls, cheerleaders, drum majorettes and tumblers to move across the field and get ready to supply the background noise and action for the scene. Three girls sleepily got up off the grass and carried their beer cans with them toward the grandstand.

Thompson said, "Now I want broad cheering (and some of the broads were certainly worth cheering) for this shot as Shirley makes her . . . uh . . . touchright."

There was a small conference on the field involving Thompson, Director of Photography Shamroy, Dawson and a young man clad only in a bathing suit. He was Loren James, Shirley's stunt double. Quickly, the players took their positions, and James ran through the scene, helping Shamroy and Thompson spot the best angles for cutbacks and missed tackles. Shirley arrived with a pink face, red lips, eyelashes as long as any of the camels' and fingernails like Fawzian scimitars. She followed her double through the run, trotting, while Dawson shouted at the Notre Dame defenders to fall down, stumble and collide. Scott Brady came up and told Shirley, "If you make this touchdown, baby, you'll be awarded the game ball."

It was never made clear whether the run was being made on a punt, kickoff or direct pass from the center. But that was incidental. Shirley stood on her own goal, somebody gave her a ball, the players scattered everywhere and she started running.

"Yeeeii!" said Shirley, as Glenn Wilder dived past her, crumpling to earth.

"Whoops!" she said, as Craig Chudy rolled under her, forcing her to take a slight hurdle.

"Oh, God!" she yelled, as Jim Martin thundered past, carefully stumbling and outgroaning a camel.

All over the field for the full 100 yards, on camera and off, Arabs and Fighting Irish barged together, and Shirley emerged into the clear to sprint the last few yards.

"Great," said Director Thompson. "Now we'll do it again." And again. And again. With each take, half-back MacLaine's broken-field ability got better and halfback MacLaine got braver.

"Come at me faster," she told Dawson. "I coulda outrun you easy that last time."

To the hulking Martin, she shouted, "Make it scary!"

If Shirley had been making the last few runs for Darrell Royal, the University of Texas coach could not have been more pleased. Each run grew faster, each leap over a falling tackler more aggressive, each sidestep or cutback through the green jerseys more adept. With every improvement, the Notre Dame players took more dangerous shots at the runner than before.

At the end of the sequence Shirley had run about two thousand yards and still had not scored. That was because William Peter Blatty's script prevented it. Shirley scored the winning touchdown in *Goldfarb* only after Scott Brady came off the Notre Dame bench in wretched anger and tackled her on the one-foot line. Then Shirley suddenly got blown over the goal when another Fawzian gusher came in, courtesy of the special-effects crew, and a dye-covered double — who was hoisted by a wire, Peter Pan style — up and into the end zone.

But long before this finally happened, halfback Shirley MacLaine had scored with the cast and crew, who were as amazed at her stamina as they were by her stiff-arms.

"You should've had seventeen years of ballet to get ready for this," said Shirley. "And a couple of Bloody Marys."

"The Rams need you," said Dawson.

"Not to put down the whole smear," said Richard Crenna, interrupting, "but the Rams could probably use all of us."

In the end there was still one thing about *Goldfarb* that bothered Jim Martin, the best nontackler half-back MacLaine would ever see.

"I played four years for Notre Dame, from forty-six through forty-nine, and we never lost a game," he said. "This is the first one we ever blew."

Well, that's show biz, Jim.

# 7

## Linebackers Have More Fun

*A couple of brutes named Butkus and Nobis.*

IT might have occurred to a lot of people in the 1960's that if every college football team had a linebacker like Tommy Nobis of Texas or Dick Butkus of Illinois, then surely all fullbacks were destined to wind up being three feet tall and singing soprano. Nobis and Butkus were special sorts of brutes whose peculiar talents were mashing ball carriers into funny shapes and sizes. What they were, in fact, were products of an era — an era that saw the position they played properly glamorized by such primates as Sam Huff and Joe Schmidt, as Bill George and Ray Nitschke. It was an era that had seen the linebacker become as big a star in college as the breakaway runner because substitution rules had fostered specialists. And the linebacker was certainly a specialist. He was the evil-looking guy who stood up noseguard to noseguard toward the opposing quarterback and looked as if he intended to mug him. On two.

Even the casual fan could tell who the linebacker was. He was the fun-lover who got to smother the runner going wide, or spear the scrambling passer drifting backward, or hit the barging plunger head-on. He was the guy who got to drop off occasionally and intercept passes, and then run in such wild-boar fashion that his coach was hard pressed to explain at the Monday boosters' luncheon why he wasn't using him on offense. The linebacker was the one player who got to show most constantly that he was the *complete* athlete; very often, the best one a team had.

Good linebackers, like Nobis or Butkus, had to be. They were the soul and heart of a defense both physically and spiritually, and just as often they were the heartthrob of a whole squad. Great ones never could *be* tired or *look* tired. They could never *not* get up from a heap, *not* hustle to the sideline, *not* be alert enough to call the defensive signals, and *not* be enthusiastic enough to keep the steady chatter going. Nobis and Butkus were all of this — and more. And above everything else, they were the living, breathing, bear-hugging, stick-'em-in-the-gizzle proof that linebackers, not blondes — and surely not quarterbacks — have more fun.

Butkus came first. And out in Illinois no player had created such a sensation since Old 77. Pete Elliott, who was then the coach, would like to have felt that his coaching had something to do with his linebacker's ability, but Pete was too honest to take such credit.

"He has intuition," said Elliott, whose 1963 success was traceable in part to the day he recruited Butkus. "On the first play of his first spring practice, before we had told him anything, he smelled out a screen pass and broke it up. In two seasons Dick has only been out of one screen pass. By that I mean he either diagnosed them and forced an incompletion or got there and made the tackle."

Elliott said, "He's naturally great at jamming up the middle against running plays. But somehow he manages to cover wide real good. He gets there, you know, because he wants to. Football is everything to him. When we have a workout canceled because of bad weather or something, he gets angry, almost despondent. He lives for contact."

Contact to Butkus was really only one thing: the moment of impact with the player unfortunate enough to have the ball. All of that other business, such as people bumping into him, foolishly trying to block him, he ignored. He was hurrying to the fun which, he said, consisted of "getting a good measure on a guy and stripping him down."

Linebackers, in a sense, are defensive quarterbacks. They prowl up and down the line behind their tackles and guards, anticipating where the daylight may occur so they can close it off. Their job is to secure all hatches. They must know when to gamble on a blitz — or dog or storm or shoot or blow, depending on your terminology — which is the act of a linebacker darting through a gap in the line on the snap and trying to smash a runner for a loss or smother a passer before he throws.

"I like to shoot any time I want to," said Butkus, who called Illinois' defensive signals. "Pete leaves it to me." On Illinois' normal defense it was reasonably safe for Butkus to put on the blitz because the tackles, 262-pound Archie Sutton and 234-pound Bill Minor, shared the middle responsibility with him. They too had size, agility and experience. Consequently, no team wore itself out running inside on Illinois. "I don't see why they would," said Butkus, honestly. "Archie and the others can take care of things pretty good — even if I guess wrong on a shoot."

The guess begins as soon as an enemy has broken

its huddle and the opposing quarterback has bent over to stare into Butkus's small, cold and dark eyes. "He's calling signals and I'm calling signals," said Butkus. "I look first at the formation. Then I look to see if a halfback is cheating a few inches. I look at the halfback's eyes, and then the quarterback's eyes and head. Some jokers, they throw in the first direction they look. I may decide at the last second that I'm gonna call a stunt, or that I'm gonna shoot. If I shoot the thing I hope is that I get a good angle on the runner, or if I've played the pass that I can strip the guy down and make him drop the ball. That takes it outta guys."

Butkus first began taking it out of guys as an All-America prep-school fullback at Chicago Vocational High. Even then he preferred defense and made seventy percent of his team's tackles. As a member of a full-blooded Lithuanian family of nine, growing up in a blue-collar district of Chicago's South Side, Butkus had not known many sports other than football. He used to swim some and he tried baseball, but from the eighth grade on football was it. And Big Ten football was what he always looked forward to.

"I had a lot of offers," he said, inoffensively. "But I didn't never really consider any of 'em except Illinois. Northwestern was . . . well, they ain't my kind of people. Notre Dame looked too hard. Besides, they didn't like the idea of my getting married, which I knew I was gonna do."

With casual honesty Butkus admitted he was no honor student. "If I was smart enough to be a doctor, I'd be a doctor," he shrugged. "I ain't, so I'm a football player. They got me in P.E."

Butkus and his wife, Helen, lived in a small but comfortable red-brick university apartment on the campus. It was not far from the old concrete-pillared stadium where Red Grange ran to fame and the new saucerlike assembly hall and field house that looked like an extension of some world's fair. The town of Champaign-Urbana consisted mostly of these two structures and the twenty-seven thousand students who went to classes in the lesser buildings scattered around them. Champaign-Urbana was flat and quiet and a good place to sleep in, which was what Butkus enjoyed best, next to football. While Helen went to work as a switchboard operator at the Champaign National Bank, Dick struggled to classes, including one that sounded terribly intellectual, kinesiology, the study of muscle movements. After that he napped. Then he made tackles and, when Helen came home, they watched television. "I get by in school," he said, "but I just want to play football. I admit it." It was fine with Helen. She just giggled and turned on "The Red Skelton Show." "It's been fun," she said.

The part that had not been fun to Butkus was the excessive fuss and adulation. Plaques and wrist-watches poured in when he made every All-America team, and was selected for various other individual awards. Earning them was fine, but he disliked being pressed for interviews and photographs. He especially disliked being needled by opposing players. " 'Hey, Butkus,' " he mimicked huskily. " 'You an All-American, huh?' Some jokers'll holler at you like that when you miss one." The highest honor Illinois could bestow on Butkus for not missing very many and leading the team to the Big Ten championship and a Rose Bowl victory over Washington was the school's Athlete of the Year award, or "A.O.Y," as it was popularly known around the campus. Butkus's attitude was typical.

"The A.O.Y. is a big deal," said editor Bill Nack of the *Daily Illini*. "But you know what kind of a guy Butkus is? He not only didn't care about it, he didn't even know what it was. When we called him to tell him he'd won, he said, 'What's that thing?' and then he said he couldn't attend the ceremony. And there we were with his name in seventy-two-point Gothic."

Nobis was the same type of contact lover as

Butkus, only he smiled more. He had an unusual love for the game, strength, quickness, speed, pride, instinct, coaching and ideal attitude — all of those things — and he, more than Butkus, might well have been the best linebacker in the history of college football.

Granted, that is a statement to rattle several plaques in the corridors of the Hall of Fame at Rutgers and encourage a lot of guys — Doak, the Ghost, Old 98, Bronko, Ernie — to maybe wonder what Tommy Nobis would have done with *their* hip feints and stiff arms. But Darrell Royal knew.

"He'd have stuffed 'em," said Royal as calmly and assuredly as you please. "All he does every week is play a great game, and you can just see joy on his face when he's out there. He's done it from the first game he started, which was as quick as I could get him into a suit as a sophomore. Players keep getting smarter, stronger and faster, and Tommy is only the latest. Aside from his super ability, he's just one of those trained pigs you love. He'll laugh and jump right in the slop for you."

Nobis, who was alert and wide-eyed on the field rather than the snarling prototype football brute, jumped in the slop enough to be judged a bona fide Southwest Conference immortal before he was even a senior. A Texas football immortal is usually any letterman who has been out of school a year, but Nobis was for real. He was a two-way all-conference guard as a sophomore in 1963 on Texas's unbeaten national championship team. That was a team led by Tackle Scott Appleton, who became Lineman of the Year. "Scott was a great defensive player," Royal said, "but when he went one-on-one against Nobis he got stuffed." In the Cotton Bowl game against Navy and Roger Staubach, concluding that season, Nobis draped himself around the Heisman Trophy winner like a clawing necklace all afternoon as Texas won a laugher, 28–6, and his performance prompted Army coach Paul Dietzel to call him "the finest linebacker I've ever seen in college." Then in 1964, playing both ways and making All-America, Nobis bulled and quicked his way to more than twenty individual tackles — most of them near the scrimmage line — in each game against Army, Oklahoma, Arkansas, SMU and Baylor, and nearly every Texas writer ran out of exclamation points.

And then in the Orange Bowl in those unbearable moments down on the Texas goal line, as the Long-horns clung to a 21–17 lead over Alabama and Joe Namath tried to take the Crimson Tide in with three plays from the one, it was Nobis again. Well, it was everybody, really, for as Royal said, "The film shows that not only did Namath not get across, but no

*Alabama lineman* got across." But it was mostly Nobis, *securing* the ballcarrier. When Nobis shut out All-America halfback Donny Anderson for the third straight year (three games: seventy-one yards), it was a feat that tickled Royal more than his collection of Roger Miller records. "He didn't drink a drop against us," said Royal. The result of all this was that when twenty-five leading newspapermen and coaches in the Southwest were polled to name the greatest defender in the history of the conference — a task they did not take frivolously, football being more important down there than elections and border disputes — Tommy Nobis was the winner.

But more important to Nobis and his teammates, as well as thousands of exes around the vast state of Texas, was the fact that he had played on winning teams. "That," said Nobis, "is what you play for — to try to be the best. Losin' is just terrible, and if anybody's got any *man* in him at all, he'll go 'til he drops tryin' not to."

"I'll tell you," said Nobis. "That's what it's all about. Whoever loses feels some real shame — I mean *shame.* That's the way it is. Boy, I hate to look at the game film on Monday. I just worry all the time about those films. I just know that I dogged it somewhere and my team will see it. I start worryin' when the game's over, and I don't stop until Monday afternoon. Heck, I get tired in a game. Everybody does. That's why I talk to myself out there. I just keep tellin' myself don't dog it, don't dog it, *please* don't dog it."

Nobis wouldn't know how to dog it if he had four legs, a wagging tail and a bowl in front of him. Neither the players nor the coaches had to look at a game film to be certain either. For example. Assistant coach Mike Campbell made phone calls to an Austin radio station for a five-minute interview after each game. Once he was in the midst of the interview after a game, and he naturally said Nobis played "great." "How do you know?" asked the announcer. "You haven't graded the films." Campbell said, "Because he always does."

The assurance that Nobis was going full out on every play did not exactly blunt the rest of Texas's defenders, among whom there were other good ones — end Pete Lammons, tackle Diron Talbert, linebacker Freddy Edwards — who tried to play a game called Beat Nobis to the Ball. Defensive back Jimmy Helms was asked how he played the pass, what tips he looked for, what moves and all that. "Aw," he said. "I just watch Nobis. He's where everything is."

Even in the spring it was true. Nobis passed up a midsemester vacation to stay in Austin and get in the proper condition for *spring* training, a rite that is

usually deemed as much fun for proven athletes as a
lecture on John Stuart Mill. But Nobis realized that
most of Royal's coaching was done in the spring, and
there would, after all, be some action. "Tommy is one
of those people who is really sort of unhappy unless
he's tackling somebody," said quarterback Marvin
Kristynik, who was Nobis's roommate.

There sure was some tackling in Texas's spring
game in which Kristynik and Nobis divided the
squad between them. Most of it was by the linebacker. Once, in a violent, three-play spasm, Nobis
slammed ballcarriers out of bounds on *opposite* sidelines for no gain, and then he intercepted a pass. One
of the runners he literally dazed was Kristynik, who
finally got up and smiled and turned to Royal, saying, "It's true, Coach. Tommy's an All-America."

Up in the press box that evening where a gaggle of
conference newspapermen was covering the game —
they do that in Texas; they *cover* spring games and
write for days about them — Longhorn publicist
Jones Ramsey was questioned on why he thought
Nobis was putting forth so much effort in so mean-
ingless a contest; why he would risk injury.

"Well," said Ramsey, "it's the only game we got
scheduled today."

As a defender, Nobis could not have played for a
man more dedicated to the virtues of sharp, funda-

mental line play than Darrell Royal — or in a system where it was better taught. Royal and his top aide, Mike Campbell, had been together for years, and they were still young. Young enough, in fact, to keep changing their methods and organization with the times. "If we coached the way we did five years ago, or even two years ago, I'll guarantee you, they'd have our gunnysacks," said Royal. Change came in the subtleties — timing, technique — that the spectator seldom can detect. It came with working on new tricks for old traps, better ways to read plays, simplifying assignments, improved drills to defeat a block and reach the ballcarrier.

"We don't teach stunts," Royal said. "Oh, we know a few to stir some folks up now and then, but on defense we teach 'em to meet the guy and try to whip him and get to that ball. Take Nobis. He doesn't key on anybody. He plays the ball and, man, does he love it when one of our ends turns somebody back into him. I can't think of anything he likes better. Me, too. But these things are taught by Mike and the rest. I'm the pride coach."

Tommy Nobis talked longer than most Texas captains had before because he was the *unofficial* self-appointed pride coach. He had so much pride and took his football so seriously in high school in San Antonio, for example, that he got up at 5:30 every morning, rode a bus, transferred, rode another, then walked, just to attend Thomas Jefferson High (the school that produced Kyle Rote) even though another school was located only a few blocks from his home.

"In San Antone you can attend any high school you want to," Tommy explained in Suite 160 of Moore-Hill Hall, an actual captain's *suite*, fixed up by Royal for Nobis and complete with hi-fi, TV, a living room, bedroom, view of Memorial Stadium and burnt-orange carpet, no less. "Jefferson had the best coach [Pat Shannon] in town, I thought, and the best program, and it was worth it to go there."

A freckled, pink-faced, red-haired, soft-voiced senior studying speech and physical education — he wouldn't cop out by claiming he was anything but a P.E. major — Nobis said honestly, "See, football is my life. It always was. I want to be a coach. You go to college for a lot of reasons, to be an engineer or a lawyer or a doctor, or something like that. And you study hard to become successful. I study and go to classes so I can play football. Football is my work, what I want to be. Now, if I'm not good enough in school, I can't *play* football. Shoot, I'm pretty poor in a lot of subjects, but I like history, it's interesting, and it's just that I have to stay after it to make decent grades. It's gettin' harder and harder to get into a good university like Texas, and harder to stay in. I try never to miss classes. It shows I'm interested and tryin'."

Nobis's pride made him an easy recruit for Texas. All it took was one visit to Oklahoma. "I knew," he said, "that either Coach Royal or Bud Wilkinson would be the two best men to play for — if I wanted to become a coach. So I went up to visit OU, but you know what? I got real mad hearin' some of those guys talk bad about Texas. I guess the pride just came out in me."

The pride was a source of worry to Nobis as well as satisfaction. He rarely trusted himself with a date after a game. "I'm just no fun then," he said. "And I don't want to take it out on some poor girl. Mostly, I just visit with my folks and get something to eat and then try to listen to some good country music and go to sleep. Dad gum it, though, the radio keeps comin' on with football scores, and I get all fired up again."

He was especially fired up at being a captain. He felt the responsibility deeply, held repetitious meetings in Suite 160 with teammates to make sure everyone was "thinking right," and, more than ever before, refused to appear weary on the field.

"You got to look a man in the eye, whether he's on your side or the other," he said. When Nobis, who was called Rancher by the team, said this he sounded a

little like a gunslinger, which is what he resembled in
the Stetson hat he occasionally wore and shirts that
wouldn't button around his mighty neck. "Look him
in the eye and let him know you're ready," he said.
"When I call a defense I stare at our guys the best I
know how to show 'em I got confidence."

Then he stared at the enemy and girded himself
up for a manner of tackling that had become the
vogue of college play, and was performed better by
Nobis than by anyone else. Players not so long ago
were taught to hit a runner low, the lower the better.
No more. Royal had taught his Longhorns, and
others had followed, to keep their heads high and go
after the man from the waist up, driving their helmets into the runner, smothering him and hoping to
jar loose the ball. Pass defenders had a simple rule:
punish the receiver for every ball he caught.

"You don't get fooled as much if you go high," said
Nobis, whose personal talent for the bear hug and
headgear-in-the-chest — "in the gizzle," he said —
had become as familiar a sight in the Southwest as
Sam Baugh's passes ever were. "You're not tryin' to
hurt anybody. Nobody wants to do that. It's just the
best way to tackle, the surest way."

Away from the fierceness of football, Tommy
Nobis could pass for a biology student who collected
butterflies. Quick-smiling, friendly, good-natured and

sensitive ("He'd be the last guy in a street fight," said Royal), he even had a sense of humor, which was fairly unusual for someone who went around sticking people in the gizzle on Saturdays. Once Nobis gave a luncheon talk to a downtown Austin civic group, and he spoke interestingly for over an hour. A couple of his teammates were present, and they were astounded.

"Hey, Tommy," said one. "I didn't know you were a *speaker*, man."

Nobis grinned, his neck exploding to size 23, and said, "What'd you think I was — just another pretty face?"

# 8

## Game of the Decade

*Tying one for the Gipper.*

Cheer, cheer for old Notre Dame,
*Equal* the echoes, *deadlock* her name,
*Draw* a volley cheer on high,
*Level* the thunder from the sky.
What though the odds be *even* or small?
Old Notre Dame will *tie* over all,
While her loyal sons are marching
Onward to victory.

**T**HAT is not exactly what the reverberating fight song says to do, of course, but that is how the big game ended every time you replayed it, and that is how several million very cranky college football fans would remember it. What the Fighting Irish did was, they tied one for the Gipper.

For fifty-nine minutes out there in overwrought East Lansing, Michigan, on the infamous Saturday of November 19, 1966, the savages of Notre Dame and Michigan State pounded each other into enough mistakes to fill Bubba Smith's uniform but the chaotic deadlock that destiny seemed to be demanding had a strange noble quality to it. And then, horribly, it didn't have that anymore.

For the people who watched it under the cold, dreary clouds of the Spartans' stadium or in their cozy living rooms on national television, something obscene happened. It might have made sense to Notre Dame. It might have been the percentage gambit. In the terror of the moment, it might have seemed like the only sane and logical thing to do, and Ara Parseghian would be willing to carry the argument that he was right throughout the rest of his career as a coach and up to that great line plunge in the sky.

But all anyone knew was that quite suddenly there at the end, the Game of the Decade suffered this enormous emptiness for which the Fighting Irish would be forever blamed.

You could forget everything else that had happened during that afternoon, all of the ferocious thudding in the line that created five fumbles, four interceptions, twenty-five other incompletions, assorted bobbles and interludes of hysteria that resulted in confusing time-outs, sideline arguments and a total of twenty rushing plays which either lost yardage or gained none, and forget the few good plays — the passes that connected. Put the nation's No. 1 team, Notre Dame, on its own 30-yard line, first down, plenty of time-outs left, momentum going, with ample room on the clock for passing. A No. 1 team, especially Notre Dame, will try *something* to stay that way, won't it?

Notre Dame did not. For reasons that it will rationalize as being more valid than they perhaps were under the gigantic circumstances, the Irish let the air out of the ball, and rode out the clock. Even as the Michigan State defenders taunted them and called the time-outs that the Irish should have been calling, Notre Dame ran into the line, the place where the big game had been hopelessly played all afternoon. No one really expected a verdict in that last desperate moment. But everybody expected Notre Dame to try, as Michigan State had tried. And when the Irish gouged at the line, the Spartans were justified in considering it a minor surrender.

"We couldn't believe it," said George Webster, Michigan State's tough roverback. "When they came up for their first play we kept hollering, 'Watch the pass, watch the pass.' But they ran. We knew the next one was a pass for sure. But they ran again. We were stunned. Then it dawned on us. They were settling for ten to ten."

You could see the Spartans jeering at the Irish down there. They had their hands on their hips, their jaws jutting out. Thoroughly disdainful. On the Michigan State sideline, players waved their arms in a gesture of "Get off the field if you've given up." And at the scrimmage line, the Spartans teased the Irish.

"I was saying, 'You're going for the tie, aren't you? You're going for the tie,'" said Webster. "And you know what? They wouldn't even look at us. They just turned their backs and went to the huddle."

Bubba Smith had hollered, "Come on, sissies. You gonna quit?" And he had yelled at Ara Parseghian, the Notre Dame coach, in the same manner. So had the other Spartan defenders.

Parseghian had made the decision to end the so-called Game of the Decade this way. His players had only followed instructions, some of them reluctantly.

"We'd fought hard to come back from ten points down and tie it up," Ara argued later. "I didn't want to risk giving it to them cheaply. One reckless pass and it could have cost us the game. I wasn't going to do a jackass thing like throw it away at this point."

Thus ended a game that had been blown up for weeks into the biggest collegiate spectacle in twenty years. Notre Dame had won eight games, lost none, and was rated No. 1. Michigan State had won nine

games, lost none, and was rated No. 2. The last game
to create such a prekickoff frenzy had also involved
Notre Dame. That was in 1946 at Yankee Stadium
when the Irish met Army. That Game of the Decade
had also brought together undefeated, untied teams
with tickets going for $100, and it had been full of as
many fluky things as this one. It too had ended in a
tie, o to o, with both teams claiming No. 1, and it had
left thousands dissatisfied and somewhat bewildered
by the fact that such folklore characters as Johnny
Lujack and George Connor, and Glenn Davis and
Doc Blanchard, had not been able to perform the
one remarkable deed that would have decided it.

Like that one years before, the East Lansing game
was decided a bushel of times, it seemed, as the two
national powers heaped heroics onto boners, and
vice versa — as Michigan State surged to a 10–0 lead
and as Notre Dame struggled back to the indecisive
tie that was earned but unapplauded.

The game was marked by all of the brutality you
somehow knew it would be when such animals were
to be present as Michigan State's 6-foot-7, 285-pound
Bubba Smith, "the intercontinental ballistic Bubba,"
as Spartan rooters referred to him, a creature whose
play at defensive end had long ago encouraged students to wear buttons that said KILL, BUBBA, KILL.

Bubba killed, all right. He killed Notre Dame's

talented sophomore quarterback, Terry Hanratty, early in the first quarter. Hanratty's passing to another whiz of a sophomore, Jim Seymour, had whirled Notre Dame into No. 1 in the first place. They had become known as the Baby Bombers. But now Hanratty was just another injured player, thanks to Bubba. As Terry had slid off right tackle on a keeper play, Bubba had whomped him in the left shoulder and separated it. It looked as if Hanratty had been smacked by a giant swinging green door.

"That didn't help us any," Bubba said later. "It just let 'em put in that Coley O'Brien, who's more slippery and faster than Hanratty. He gave us more trouble. Hanratty sits there and waits to throw, and that's what our defense wanted. We knew we could get to him."

Given a choice, of course, Ara Parseghian would have preferred to play the rest of the game with Hanratty at quarterback. He could throw deep better than O'Brien, although O'Brien threw well enough to gain the tie. Ara not only would have liked to have had Hanratty but his All-America halfback, Nick Eddy, and his center, George Goeddeke, as well. Like Hanratty, Goeddeke, a fine blocker, went out with a first-quarter injury, compliments of Bubba. It was an ankle. But Eddy, a great broken field runner, never even got in the game. The Grand Trunk got Eddy.

The Grand Trunk was not another nickname for Bubba Smith. It was the railroad train that Notre Dame took from South Bend to East Lansing the day before the game. When the train arrived, Eddy slipped off the steps — hardly a tribute to his cutting and swerving — and fell onto an already injured shoulder. He was out. And sophomore Bob Gladieux was told in a doomsday Parseghian voice that he would start the biggest game of 1966 at left half.

As Notre Dame still lives with the tie, it has not forgotten these injuries and the alibis they strongly suggest. Still, as Michigan State coach Duffy Daugherty said, the Irish do not exactly substitute with girls from Sweet Briar. O'Brien and Gladieux could play for most anybody, he said. And even Parseghian admitted, "Considering everything, I thought they played super."

Indeed they did. They weren't in the game very long before they got Notre Dame untracked. On a marvelously executed play, O'Brien, a young man who required two insulin shots a day for diabetes, shot a thirty-four-yard spiral to Gladieux for a touchdown in the second quarter. Gladieux was cutting behind a defender right at the goalpost and never broke stride. Until that play, which narrowed the score to 10–7, Notre Dame was not even on the field.

The combination of Eddy's injury, which everyone tried to keep secret, and the mounting pressure of the game made Notre Dame an extraordinarily grim-looking group when the Irish arrived in East Lansing. Usually loose and smiling, the Irish marched into the Jack Tar Hotel beneath a marquee that said WELCOME TO THE BIG ONE with frozen, dedicated expressions that for some indescribable reason did not suggest confidence. Jim Seymour, the startling young pass catcher and friendly, outgoing personality of other Saturdays, was rigid, quiet and uncommunicative. In the battle itself Seymour was double covered so well all day that he was scarcely noticeable. He had one decent chance at a pass but dropped it.

The Irish should have been happy to leave South Bend, even on the Grand Trunk, after the week of agonizing attention they got. Being the favorite, being No. 1, and of course being Notre Dame, the Irish on Monday were asked to greet hordes of reporters and photographers from everywhere. The number would swell each day. It was almost the same for Michigan State. Both Parseghian and Daugherty had to hold daily press conferences and play the game over and over ahead of time. And what could they say? It was an honor and a privilege to be involved in a thing like this, that's all.

Nothing was hinted at either in interview or work-outs that would tip the game off. Both teams were so talented and physically imposing, and had beaten their opponents so easily, it was impossible to fore-tell how the game would go. Neither could run much, you figured, but both might be able to pass if their quarterbacks had a spare second to get the ball away. No one wanted a freak play — a fumble, an interception, a penalty — to decide it. Everybody wanted a clear winner. The last thing anyone thought about was a tie. No, that was the next to last thing. The last thing was all of the mistakes that occurred.

For a long while, it seemed the two teams would never calm down and look like the No. 1 and the No. 2 that they were supposed to be. Of the four passes Terry Hanratty tried before his shoulder met Bubba Smith, three were atrociously off target, one of them a routine screen that darted into the turf. The run-ners, meanwhile, went nowhere, primarily because of Bubba and George Webster of the Spartans, and of Kevin Hardy and Jim Lynch of the Irish. When Notre Dame failed to get off a punt because of a poor snapback, Michigan State countered with a fumble, a delay penalty, a clip, and interference on a fair catch. It looked like the big intramural game at Dartmouth.

One interesting thing had happened, though, in the midst of all these plays that did nothing but backfire. On an aborted sprintout pass by Michigan State's quarterback, Jimmy Raye, a flighty junior with a mustache, Duffy had seen something. Split end Gene Washington, one of the surest and fastest receivers in the country, had beaten his coverage by ten yards. Washington, who was the Big Ten hurdles champion, could outrun most people.

"I can look in a man's eyes and know whether I can beat him," Washington explained afterward. "I knew I could beat those guys all day."

Near the end of the first quarter, with a first down at his own 27, Raye called the play again. He skittered out to the right, stopped, and let sail a long one. Washington took it over his shoulder and fell out of bounds at the Notre Dame 31. Nine battering ground plays later, with merciless double-team blocking on Kevin Hardy, the Spartans scored. Regis Cavendar, who had come in for Bob Apisa at fullback, crashed over, and it was 7–0.

On their next possession in the second quarter, the Spartans scored again. Raye, who was from South Carolina — another of the brilliant blacks who escaped Dixie — danced away for a thirty-yard gain, and he then hit Washington, a tall black athlete from LaPorte, Texas, for seventeen more yards. Two passes and a run failed, so the Spartans settled on barefoot placekicker Dick Kenney's field goal to make it 10–0.

Although it continually appeared as if it might, Michigan State never got beyond Notre Dame's 47-yard line for the remainder of the day. Johnny Ray, Notre Dame's big, boom-voiced defensive coach, felt he knew why. "We weren't getting out of our tracks in the first half," he said. "Maybe we were tight. Anyhow, we told our kids to forget everything and just start hitting people."

There was much to say for Notre Dame's defense, which was led by Jim Lynch, the linebacker, and Kevin Hardy, the hulking tackle. On no less than sixteen rushing plays it held the Spartans to no gain or minus-yardage. It held Clinton Jones, as good a runner as 1966 produced, to thirteen yards on ten carries and this seemed like the equivalent to stopping Cassius Clay at mid-punch. Jones and Lynch once came together in the loudest collision of the afternoon. It occurred when Lynch picked off a Jimmy Raye pass and stormed upfield only to be met by Jones at the knees. The blow turned Lynch a complete, soaring flip. He landed on his golden headgear, fumbled, and Jones recovered. The dizzy play,

one of many, enabled Michigan State to keep possession and subsequently to get its field goal.

It was late in the third quarter that Coley O'Brien
revved up the tying drive. He hit passes over the
middle and out in the flats, and short, stabbing runs
by Larry Conjar, the fullback, Rocky Bleier, a halfback, and O'Brien himself moved the ball to Michigan State's 10-yard line. There, it was third and
three — the kind of play that made Ara Parseghian
chew his gum on the sideline like a rabbit. The call
was a pass, but George Webster and Bubba Smith
applied so much pressure on O'Brien he did well to
scamper back to the line of scrimmage. The Irish
thus cashed in on a field goal by Joe Azzaro.

By now, with a slow kind of subtlety, the look of
the game had changed. Michigan State, certainly the
better team in the first half, did not seem so sure
anymore. Notre Dame had fought back. It was all
even. And now some freaky break would decide it,
and surely the wrong team would win. Whoever it
was would be wrong. You knew that.

Right away, the play that *should* have turned the
game did in fact happen. Jimmy Raye, escaping a
rush, threw a wild pass — the Spartans were gam-
bling, unlike the Irish — and Notre Dame's safety,
Tom Schoen, stole it. He rambled back thirty-one
yards with it to the Spartans' 18-yard line. At this

point, anyone who thought Ara would try anything other than three line plunges and a winning field goal should have been locked up in intensive care.

The Irish did run on first down. Larry Conjar made two yards. Fine. Second down at the 16. But now what was this? Here was Dick Haley, a substitute halfback, taking a pitchout and going wide to the left and drifting backwards. And here came Bubba Smith and another Spartan, Phil Hoag, rumbling through to smother him for an eight-yard loss. So it was third down back on the 24. O'Brien failed with a pass, then, and it was fourth down and Joe Azzaro's kick had to travel forty-two yards. It was wide to the right, and the swoon of relief in Spartan Stadium made the structure lean a little.

Notre Dame had got the big break and blown it.

"That Haley play," said Parseghian. "That was just leakage. We leaked a guy through, blew an assignment." He stared at the dressing room floor. "Damn," he said.

Back outside, as the thousands filed through the stadium tunnels, a Michigan State coed looked blankly at her boyfriend and back up at the scoreboard. It still said 10 to 10. "Damn," she said. "Damn, damn, damn."

In the aftermath of the game of the decade, everyone had something quaint to say. Ara Parseghian still claimed No. 1 for his team (Notre Dame did in fact win most of the popularity polls), saying, "When you're Number One and you only get tied, you can't lose it."

Duffy Daugherty had other views. "We ought to be Number One and Notre Dame ought to be Number One A," he said.

And Bear Bryant, whose splendid Alabama team wound up with an 11–0 record after demolishing Nebraska in the Sugar Bowl, had still another idea.

"I have a lot of seniors on this team," said Bryant. "Some of them will be graduating and going on over to Vietnam, I suppose. When they get there, I just hope they don't play for a tie."

With second thoughts then, the Bear said, "But you know what. Playing that old tie must have been the right thing to do. All I know is, Ara wound up with Number One."

As a Spartan coed would say, Damn, damn, damn if he didn't.

# 9

## The Arm

*A sweet life for Broadway Joe.*

S TOOP-SHOULDERED and sinisterly handsome, he slouched against the wall of the saloon, a filter cigarette in his teeth, collar open, perfectly happy and self-assured, gazing through the uneven darkness to sort out the winners from the losers. As a couple of neat ones came by wearing miniskirts, net stockings, big false eyelashes, long pressed hair and soulless expressions, he grinned approvingly and said, "Hey, hold it, man — foxes." It was Joe Namath at play, studying the defensive tendencies of New York's off-duty secretaries, stewardesses, dancers, nurses, bunnies, actresses, shopgirls — all of the people who made life stimulating for a bachelor who could throw the best pass in pro football. Sitting there, he seemed to pose a question for us all:

Would you rather be young, single, rich, famous, talented, energetic and happy — or President?

Joe Namath was not to be fully understood by most of us, of course. We were ancient, being over twenty-three, and perhaps a bit arthritic, seeing as how we couldn't do all those dances. We weren't comfortably tuned in to the Jefferson Air Freight — or whatever their names were. We had not-so-skinny trousers and pockets we could get our hands into. But Joe was not pleading to be understood. He was youth, success, the clothes, the car, the penthouse, the big town, the girls, the autographs and the games on Sundays. He simply was. The best we could do was catch a slight glimpse of him as he sped by us in this life, and hope that he would in some way help prepare us for the day when we would surely elect public officials who wore beanies and had term themes to write.

Whatever Joe meant to himself behind his wisecracks, his dark, rugged good looks, and his flashy tailoring, he was mostly one thing — a big celebrity in a celebrity-conscious town. This added up to a lot of things, some desirable, some not. It meant a stack of autographs everywhere he went ("Hey Joe, for a friend of mine who's a priest, a little somethin' on the napkin, huh?"), a lot of TV and radio stuff, a lot of photography stills for ads and news and continual interviews with the press. Such things he handled with beautiful nonchalance, friendliness — and lip.

Then came the good part. It meant he got to sit at one of those key tables in Toots Shor's — 1 and 1A — the ones just beyond the partition from the big circular bar where everyone from Des Moines could watch him eat his prime rib. It meant that when he hit P. J. Clarke's the maître d' in the crowded back room, Frankie Ribando, would always find a place for him, while, out front, waiter Tommy Joyce, one of New York's best celebrity-spotters, would tell everyone, "Joe's inside." It meant he could crawl into the pubs during the late hours when the Copa girls and the bunnies were there having their after-work snacks, even though the line at the door might stretch from Second Avenue to the Triborough Bridge, places long ago ruled impenetrable by earth people, or nonmembers of the youth cult.

Easing into the clubs and restaurants that he frequented, Joe handled his role well. "Don't overdo it, man," he said. "I can hang around till three or four and still grab my seven or eight." He sat, he ate, he sipped, he smoked, he talked, he looked, and maybe he scared up a female companion and maybe he didn't. "I don't like to date so much as I just like to kind of, you know, run into somethin'," he said.

Namath was unlike all of the super sports celebri-

ties who came before him in New York — Babe
Ruth, Joe DiMaggio and Sugar Ray Robinson, to
name three of the more obvious. They were *grown
men* when they achieved the status he now enjoyed.
Might even be wearing hats. They were less hip to
their times and more or less aloof from the crowd.
Joe had thrust himself into the middle of it. Their
fame came more slowly — with the years of earning
it. Joe Namath was a happening.

He happened first when he was a sophomore passing star who made Alabama coach Bear Bryant
change his offense. He happened again as a junior
when he proved to be such an away-from-the-field
mover that Bryant had to kick him off the team for
drinking and carousing before the last two games of
the season. He happened again when he returned to
take Alabama to the 1964 national championship on
a gimpy leg. Then Sonny Werblin, the owner of the
New York Jets, made him *really* happen when he
gave him that $400,000, the check that changed all
of football and brought about the NFL-AFL merger,
on the second day of 1965. No football player in history had ever been worth half that much. But this
wasn't all. He quickly had to undergo an operation
on his knee to have a torn cartilage removed and a
loose ligament tied. And, thanks to those splendid

satirists, Robert Benton and David Newman, the hip line in New York became, "Sorry I can't make your party, Sybil, but I'm going to the probing of Joe Namath's knee."

Werblin had known something about timing. Taking advantage of Namath's exposure in an exciting Orange Bowl game in which he had sparkled heroically even though his Alabama team had narrowly lost to Texas, 21–17, the big check came immediately in the aftermath. The game had been an utter classic, with the No. 3 Longhorns upsetting Bear Bryant's Namath-led No. 1 Crimson Tide — and all before a prime time evening television audience.

It would later be a quirk of fate that Namath would be joined on the New York Jets, and become close friends with, four members of the Texas team which defeated him. They would be George Sauer, Jr., Pete Lammons, Jim Hudson and John Elliott. Sauer had caught a touchdown pass from Hudson in the Orange Bowl game, Elliott had put a big rush on Joe, and Lammons had intercepted him twice.

"Yeah, they talk about that a lot," Joe grinned.

So Joe Namath was already an instant celebrity with his money, but his image would grow throughout 1965 when a certain amount of suspense built as to whether he would be drafted, or whether his knee would allow him to play any football at all for Werblin's $400,000. During it all, the wisecracks flowed like cocktails.

"I'd rather go to Vietnam than get married," he said as the draft board in his hometown of Beaver Falls, Pennsylvania, requested that he appear for his physical.

Then after he flunked it and a lot of superpatriots bristled, as they did at Cassius Clay, Joe said with brutal honesty, "How can I win? If I say I'm glad, I'm a traitor, and if I say I'm sorry, I'm a fool."

Once when he was asked to point out the difference between Bear Bryant and Jet Coach Weeb Ewbank, Joe grinned and said, "Coach Bryant was always thinking about winning. Weeb is mainly concerned over what kind of publicity you get."

When a writer tried to tease him about his classes at Alabama, asking if he majored in basket weaving, Joe said, "Naw, man, journalism — it was easier."

When he was asked to explain the origin of the white shoes that he wore during a game, he shot back, "Weeb ordered 'em. He thought it would save tape."

But all of this was a while ago. Now that he had proved he was worth every cent of his contract and become the quarterback that Werblin gambled he would be — a throwing artist who ranked with the best — he was still a swinger. Namath tried to be Johnny Unitas and Johnny Eager rolled into one; he was in a curious sense pro football's very own Beatle.

He lived in a penthouse on New York's upper East Side, one that featured a huge white llama-skin rug, an Italian marble bar, an elaborate stereo hookup, an oval bed that seemed to increase in size with each glance, a terrace and more roommates than he could count.

He whirled around the city in his convertible, the radio blaring, parking by fireplugs whenever possible, wearing tailor-made suits with tight pants and loud print linings, grabbing checks, laughing, enjoying life, spending maybe $25,000 a year ("on nuthin', man") and wondering why anyone should be offended.

"I believe in letting a guy live the way he wants if he doesn't hurt anyone. I feel that everything I do is okay for me, and doesn't affect anybody else, including the girls I go out with," he says. "Look man, I live and let live. I like everybody. I don't care what a man is as long as he treats me right. He can be a gambler, a hustler, someone everybody else thinks is obnoxious, I don't care so long as he's straight with me and our dealings are fair. I like Cassius Clay, Bill Hartack, Doug Sanders and Paul Hornung, all the controversial guys. They're too much. They're colorful, man. If I couldn't play football, I'd like to be a pro golfer. But I like everybody." Joe's eyes sparkled as if he was getting ready to make a joke, and he said, "Why, I even like Howard Cosell."

Joe Willie's philosophy was more easily grasped when one realized what he lifted himself up from in Beaver Falls. It is a picturesque but poor town in the hills about thirty miles outside of Pittsburgh. He was the youngest of five children, and his parents were divorced when he was in the sixth grade. His father was a mill worker. He lived with his mother, and there was little money, so Joe hustled. He shot pool, he shined shoes, he ran messages for bookies, he hustled; he got by. "Where I come from," he said, "ain't nobody gonna hustle *me.*"

As he prepared for his senior year of high school the idea of going to college was remote. An older brother, John, was a career man in the Army, a warrant officer for a time in Vietnam. Joe was set on joining the Air Force and making it a career. What stopped him was a lot of touchdown passes and offers from precisely fifty-two universities, including Notre Dame — but not Alabama.

"I wanted to go to Maryland because I was stupid enough to think it was down South," he said. "I didn't know from outside Pittsburgh, man. All I knew was that I wanted to go South. I think a lot of kids from the East and Midwest do because of the climate."

Namath took the college board exams and failed them at Maryland. "You needed seven hundred fifty and I scored seven hundred forty-five, right? They wanted me to take it again, but I said to hell with it." He thought next of Penn State, but Maryland had to play Penn State the next few seasons and didn't want to face Namath. Maryland's coaches promptly called Bear Bryant at Alabama, whom the Terps would not play, and Bear welcomed "the greatest athlete I've ever coached."

Despite his dismissal for the last two games of his junior season, Namath worshipped Alabama and his experiences and successes there. Bryant was the greatest man he had ever known, Joe even had the hint of a southern accent, his closest friends were from Alabama, and if there was anything that made him mad it was the eastern press, which he called "the northern press."

"There's only three things I'm touchy about," he said. "Number One, the northern press and how it ignores southern football when I'll guarantee you that a team like Louisiana Tech can beat about eighty of these lousy schools up North. Two is the publicity that Notre Dame gets. And three is a joke about a Hungarian."

One other tiny thing bothered him when he first went to the Jets after taking Alabama to three bowl games with seasons of 10–1, 9–2 and 10–1. He read a statement by a pro player who suggested that Joe might not want to "pay the price" with his big salary. "Can you believe that?" he said. "Why, you can't play for Bryant for four years and not know how to *pay the price* for what you get out of life."

Considering that the most money Joe ever had at one time before he signed the Jet contract was $600, which he got for peddling some Alabama game tickets, he might have been justified in blowing the whole stack on a car, a blonde and a diamond ring. He had a shrewd business consultant, however, in a Birmingham lawyer named Mike Bite. At Bite's bidding he learned to spread the money out as he would an evening on the town. He took only $25,000 a year in salary. He had $200,000 in bonuses working for him over the next one hundred years or something like that. And he was generous enough to let members of his family in on the loot. Two brothers and a brother-in-law got on the Jets' scouting payroll at $10,000 a year.

He wasn't a winner right off, of course. The Jets' 5–8–1 record his first year made New York the worst team Joe had ever played on. Admittedly, he didn't know the first thing about quarterbacking a pro team. He had the quickest delivery anyone had ever seen, and he got back into the Jets' exceedingly secure passing pocket, formed by Sherman Plunkett, Dave Herman, Sam DeLuca and Winston Hill — his "bodyguards" — so fast that Kansas City's All-AFL lineman, Jerry Mays, said, "He makes the rush obsolete." But there was so much he had to learn.

At Alabama he had raced back only five yards and released the ball in approximately 1.3 seconds. Ewbank, however, demanded that he get eight yards deep and go 3.2 seconds before throwing. His firmly braced knee prevented him from using the threat of the run, which he had done so well for two and a half seasons in Tuscaloosa.

He had to learn how to read defenses, how to look for tips among the defensive backs, how to hit his receivers on the break, how to set up when he threw, how to call audibles and how to convince his Jet teammates that he could lead them.

"At first," said defensive end Gerry Philbin, "there was an undercurrent of resentment — nothing you could pinpoint, but it was there — about Joe's money and his publicity. That was at first. It disappeared when everybody found out what a great guy he is."

Curley Johnson, the punter, said, "Mainly we

wanted to see how good he was. He really didn't throw the ball that damn well for a long time. Then, we knew how good he was — the best."

Said the ace receiver, Don Maynard, "At first he'd knock us over on short patterns. But he slacked off. His timing got great, and he adjusted to situations like a veteran." To this, George Sauer, Jr., another top Jet receiver, added, "He never knew how to throw on the break. The ball was always early or late. Now it's there."

Not according to Joe, though. "I haven't thrown well since Alabama," he said. "Maybe it's my leg. I don't know. If I knew, I'd throw better. You hear a lot about getting the ball up here by your ear, but that's junk. It doesn't matter how you deliver as long as the ball goes where you aim it and gets there when it's supposed to. I don't know *how* I throw the ball, and I don't remember anybody ever teaching me to throw it. But there's a lot I *did* find out pretty quick."

For one thing, Joe said, the quarterback who has to call a pile of audibles (changing plays at the line of scrimmage) is a dumb one. "You're supposed to know what the defense will be when you're in the huddle. I'll only call five or six audibles a game now. At first it was more. That's funny, too, because the public thinks it's a big deal if a quarterback can switch plays a lot at the scrimmage line. They think it makes him brainy. Most of the time it means he's stupid."

A simple thing it took Joe a season to learn was that backs key on the mannerisms of a quarterback and cover their areas accordingly.

"For example," he said, "about eighty percent of the time when the quarterback takes the snap, turns and races back to set up with his back to the defense, he'll throw to the right. That's because it's easier, more natural, to plant your feet when you start that way. On the other hand, it's easier to throw left when you drop straight back, without turning around. There are defensive backs who'll play you for this and, of course, you have to cross 'em up."

Strangely enough, Joe found that the ball had a tendency to turn wrong on his home turf of Shea Stadium. "It's my unfavorite place to play," said he. "Somehow, the wind swirls in there, and I don't like what it does to the balls I throw. It could be some kind of fixation, I don't know. Like I have about throwing a night football. It's different, I swear. The coaches and the sporting goods salesmen say it's the same ball, but it isn't. It goes different. So does the ball in Shea."

If there is a single myth that Joe Namath would like to have destroyed about pro football, it is the widely held belief that the game's quarterbacks are pampered by opposing defensive linemen; that they are not "shot at," particularly himself because of his bad knee and what his drawing power means to the league.

"Okay," he said. "How about a Houston exhibition in Birmingham one time? Don Floyd comes at me after the whistle, and I move to miss a shot and reinjure my knee. What's that? Of course, Don didn't mean to. He says he didn't hear the whistle, and I believe him. But he was comin' at me and I kind of think he'd of hit me if he could have. What about a Denver game? I still got a sore back from that one. Johnny Bramlett, one of their linebackers, is a buddy of mine — he played for Memphis State — and he had me over to dinner the night before the game. His wife cooked an Italian feast, plenty good, too. But the next day he was after me like a tiger, and he'd cuss me when he missed. He wanted to win, man. That's the way it is. I don't think any of our opponents are too interested in my health."

If he stayed healthy, Joe Namath thought he could achieve his deepest ambition, which was "to become known as a good quarterback, not a rich one." Slowly, because trying to fathom youth is always a slow process, you got the impression that Joe was quite serious about it and, despite his hip ways, was working hard to make it. Beneath the gaudy surface there somehow beamed through a genuine, friendly and likable young man. But he was going to be himself. He was going to do it his way, and nobody else's.

And he was of course destined to jolt football like it had never been jolted by beating the Baltimore Colts — his way, which was the only way it could ever have happened. Believe it or not, Joe Namath simply *was*.

# 10

## Pursuit of a Blue Chipper

*He comes along every year — the most wanted
high school athlete ever to fasten a chin strap.*

EVERY year he turns up in some little dry-bed
town where the folks are God-fearing, mother-
loving, flag-saluting and psychoneurotic about football. He is big, tough, intelligent, unselfish, a leader.
And fast? He runs the hundred in 9.4 — uphill. He
runs the quarter in 46 flat — in the rain. And his arm?
Why, it's like one of those bazookies that we kill the
Red Commonist Nazi menace with. Everybody in
town has seen him flick the ball sixty yards on his
knees with two linebackers jerking on his face guard.
Man, if he doesn't have an arm then Joe Namath
was a dress designer. He's got it all, which is why
Ara Parseghian and Bear Bryant and Darrell Royal
and the Detroit Tigers and the Boston Celtics and
the Morgan Guaranty Trust have all been trying to

sign him up since he was in the fourth grade. And it is why whoever winds up with him will announce it in a press conference on the battleship Missouri and why those who don't will go tattling off to the NCAA, CIA, FBI and ARVN.

He goes by several familiar names, of course. He is known as the No. 1 Blue Chipper, the Prized Recruit, the Top Prospect, the Most Wanted, the Most Highly Coveted, the Leader of the Tribe, the Boss Stud, the Head Hoss.

He has had a lot of other names, too. Several years ago he was Bill De Correvont from Chicago's Austin High School, a kid who put 120,000 in Soldier Field for a city championship game. Once he was Ronnie Knox out on the West Coast. A couple of times he came out of Louisiana and was called John David Crow and Billy Cannon. But as often as not, he has risen from that holy land of high school football known as the State of Texas and he has been named things like Doak Walker, Bobby Layne and Kyle Rote.

It is sort of expected for Texas to produce a Head Hoss every few years. After all, the state has over one thousand schools playing football in an interscholastic league that permits championship playoffs in four different classifications. This enables a lot of varied parts of the vast region to go cuckoo, such as one year when the championships were won by teams from Austin in the Hill Country, Brownwood in central Texas, Plano up in the north and Tidehaven on the coast.

Outside of the large cities — Dallas, Houston and Fort Worth — high school football is just about the sole interest of everybody from the banker and the undertaker to all the guys hanging around Snap's Esso station. Coleman's Fighting Blue Cats are absolute celebrities during the season, and so are El Campo's Rice Birds, Port Lavaca's Sandcrabs, Hutto's Hippoes, Trent's Gorillas, Itasca's Wampus Cats, Cuero's Gobblers and lots of others.

Because of the vast exposure it has become almost impossible for Texas not to have at least one player emerge each fall as a near-national figure before he is ever issued a college freshman's T-shirt, a convertible and a Bluebonnet Festival queen. San Antonio's Warren McVea, for example, was certainly well known to about fifty colleges before he ever selected the University of Houston. A film of a 55–48 state playoff game that Warren starred in was already on the banquet circuit and threatening to make its way to Lincoln Center. McVea felt compelled to hold press conferences to announce he had narrowed his choice down to just twenty campuses. A year later a young man named Bill Bradley came out of Palestine

with the nickname of Super Bill, and before he chose
the University of Texas the public somehow had the
feeling that he had been forced to turn down seventeen major league baseball offers, all of them worth
$500,000 each. Not long after Bradley the village of
Bridge City finally gave a diploma to a lad named
Steve Worster, who was modestly considered to be
"the greatest power running back in Texas history."
In the midst of an ABC television special on him, the
University of Texas beat LSU in the finals for Worster, and fifty other proselyters got out their road
maps and scurried off in search of Blue Chip Prospect No. 2.

And now it was time for Texas to offer up another
phenomenon, this time a quarterback from the flat,
arid plains of Abilene. He had all the attributes that
made recruiters dance and holler — size, speed, arm,
brains, moves, family, church, statistics, leadership
and handshake. Jack Mildren was his name. He had
been throwing touchdown passes on organized teams
since the fifth grade, he had always been a winner,
he had the savvy that only the son of an ex-coach
could have, he had come from a formidable high
school with an *eight-man* coaching staff, and everybody knew about him from UCLA to West Point.

It was only natural that he would lead recruiters
on one of the merriest chases of their careers — over

farm roads, oil pumps, city streets and Astrodomes — before he would eventually put his signature on a preenrollment agreement while flashbulbs exploded and a proud family brushed away its collective tear. This is the story of that chase, which is pretty much the story of college recruiting everywhere.

It began the summer before Jack Mildren even started his senior season at Abilene Cooper High, in which he would complete 147 passes for 2,076 yards and 20 touchdowns and run for 787 more yards and 24 more touchdowns, all of it in what was generally considered to be the ruggedest "big school" league in the state, a thing called District 3-AAAA, which included a lot of the pillars of Texas schoolboy football: teams from Odessa, Midland, San Angelo and Big Spring. It was before Jack would lead the Cooper Cougars unbeaten through 13 games and right into the state finals, where they would lose 20–19 because, it would be ruled — controversially — he did not score a touchdown from the one-foot line on the last play of the game.

The way it started was that Mildren's coach, Merrill Green, a former Oklahoma player, asked Jack's father if he had any idea where his oldest son might want to go to college. Was Jack still a big SMU fan, as he had been as a youngster, or was his mind open?

Well, the father said he just hoped Jack would get some offers.

"He won't get more than one hundred," Green said. The coach then suggested that the family brace for this by taking the quarterback on an unofficial tour of some of the campuses Jack might be interested in so that he could see them without the frills of a big game weekend or without the adulation that can be poured over a kid when the recruiters notice that he is 6'1", weighs 190, passes, runs and makes nothing but A's in school.

Larry Mildren, the father, who had been a high school football coach before eventually settling down in Abilene as a salesman for a cable TV company, knew enough about recruiting to agree with Merrill Green. He honestly did not know where Jack might want to go to college. It might be SMU in Dallas, a Methodist school that would tie in with the family's religion and a school Jack had been a fan of because of Doak Walker, Kyle Rote, Don Meredith and all that. It might be TCU, the nearest campus, only one hundred fifty miles away in Fort Worth, a school enthusiastically endorsed by Jack's middle brother, Richard, who also played for Cooper. Photographs of TCU players were all over the walls of the bedroom that the brothers (and teammates) shared, leaving little space for Jack to hang the All-State and All-America plaques he would win. Or it might be Texas, the school that never lets a big one get away and was a favorite of the third and youngest brother, Glynne. Larry Mildren was only sure that it would not be Texas A&I down in Kingsville where he had played and the town where Jack had been born.

Jack was eager, of course, to see a few of the campuses in the summer, not particularly because he wanted to ask a lot of questions about their engineering departments or business courses. In a statement characteristic of most prospects, he told his father, "I just want to go somewhere I might be able to start as a sophomore and where we may have a chance to win a national championship before I get through."

Although that did not exactly narrow it down, the family decided to show the quarterback a mild variety of schools within a reasonable driving distance from Abilene. They agreed to visit Texas A&M first (320 miles), then TCU (150), then Arkansas (500), then Oklahoma (300) and then Texas (220), and do it on different weekends if possible.

The trips were made, but not exactly in the manner that Merrill Green at first had suggested. The Mildrens never were able to sneak into any town at all for a pedestrian look-around, unless one considers it sneaking to be met everywhere by the coaching staffs, and given a guided tour of every landmark from the training room to the admissions office.

Whether the visits accomplished anything for Jack or not, they served to whet the appetites of the schools. Their logic was that if Jack Mildren was interested enough in them to take a look at their campus before his senior season had even begun, then he was surely a prize to pursue.

In recruiting, a coach looks for any edge he can find, and there were ten colleges that had a perfect right to go after Mildren ahead of any other prospect. Merrill Green was indirectly responsible for three of the reasons himself. First, Green had played at Oklahoma, which justified the Sooners in being serious about him from the beginning. But Green had coached for a while at Arkansas under Frank Broyles, whom he liked and admired, and this certainly made Arkansas believe it had a chance. To complicate it further, Green had been the former roommate of, and best man for, coach Eddie Crowder at Colorado. Crowder thought his old pal might just help point Jack toward Boulder. And then, of course, there were all of these other tie-ins. Texas Tech sits out there only one hundred sixty miles northwest of Abilene. It has always been a

favorite for Abilene students. And Baylor prided itself on sending a lot of quarterbacks to the pros,
which might appeal to Jack. And one of Larry
Mildren's old friends, Jake Helms, was the freshman
coach at Texas A&M now, which could be a persuasive force. Another of the father's old friends, Emory
Bellard, was an assistant at Texas, which might be
the same. The president of the Abilene school board
was a Rice man, and that wouldn't hurt the Owls.
TCU had the bit about being the closest Southwest
Conference campus, and the family already knew
several of the TCU coaches. Finally, the family was,
after all, Methodist, which never stopped giving
SMU hope.

Sometimes a prospect can add to the complica-
tions of his ultimate decision by doing the very
natural thing of answering his mail. Soon after the
season started, Jack Mildren began receiving letters
and questionnaires from all over the country — from
Notre Dame, UCLA, Army, everywhere. If you answer them you begin to get more personal letters,
then phone calls, then requests for game films and
then visits from alumni in the area or by assistant
coaches. This suddenly sank in on Jack Mildren one
evening at home when the phone rang and it was
UCLA coach Tommy Prothro, who said, "We probably don't have a very good chance to get you, son,

but I believe that if you'll just come visit us, you'll want to stay."

There were recruiting rules in the Southwest Conference designed to keep college coaches from stumbling over each other at high school workouts — and to keep prospective athletes from stumbling over recruiters. A staff could make only two official visits to a prospect before the date on which he can sign a letter of intent binding him to that school. The date this year was February 21. Of course, accidental visits didn't count. "Bump-ins" they were called, and there were a lot of them. A bump-in was when the athlete just happens to meet up with a college coach in a public place, like, for instance, a hamburger stand where the team hung out, or a coffee shop where the father hung out, or a department store where the mother shopped. At any rate, the two-visit rule was fine for Southwest coaches to live with among themselves, but it has no effect on an outsider like Oklahoma, which happened to be located closer to a greater part of Texas than several Southwest campuses.

Not that Oklahoma ever needs anything to incur the anger of Texas schools. Long ago Bud Wilkinson started reaching into Texas for good athletes, and Oklahoma started reaching for Jack Mildren before anyone else. Maybe it was because of Merrill Green and maybe not. Maybe it was because Abilene, being a big oil town, had a lot of well-to-do and influential OU exes, and maybe not. Maybe it was because an Oklahoma coach, Barry Switzer, was practically camping on the Mildrens' front lawn, and maybe not. But on the one weekend he had free from playing a Cooper High game, Jack was invited up to Norman for an Oklahoma-Maryland game, and he went.

Everybody else howled about that later. They knew it must have made a huge impression on Mildren and would make their selling jobs even tougher. Darrell Royal put it better than anyone.

"I remember when I was a kid and went to Norman for the first time. I saw those big red helmets with white 'O' on 'em, and those big shoulder pads," said Darrell. "Why, I knew I couldn't go anywhere else. I went back to Hollis and got my radio and put it out there on the porch on Saturdays so I could listen to the OU games and play like I had on one of those red helmets as I ran around dodging trees and stiff-arming anthills."

Jack Mildren had been a good prospect on the basis of his junior year, but as his team rolled along through his senior season he became a superb prospect. The Southwest recruiters could hardly wait until the Cougars finished their campaign to start their sales pitches, though Oklahoma, of course, had already started. After one particular game Green admitted some Sooner coaches to the Abilene dressing room where the Southwest coaches couldn't go because Mildren's season wasn't over yet. Darrell Royal got especially outraged. He called the Cooper coach to tell him he was granting Oklahoma an unfair advantage.

Green apologized and said he realized he had made a mistake, but he couldn't resist teasing Royal at the same time.

"Darrell, I wonder how many proselyters can take a kid out to the LBJ Ranch?" Green asked. "That seems to me like a little bit of an unfair advantage for Texas."

The recruiting season officially opens on a Texas athlete about one second after his final game. In Jack Mildren's case his pursuers waited an extra day for the quarterback and the family to recover from the heart-wracking loss to Austin Reagan in the finals at TCU stadium in Fort Worth. Jack had not played his best that day, although he passed for two touchdowns and ran for one and gave his Cougars a 19–7 lead that they blew. It was a very sad afternoon for Abilene. Nothing in life ever seems quite so monumental as that great big high school loss or victory.

So the recruiters sort of stood back and stayed away from the downcast Abilene players after the game. They hung their heads like the families did and dug their toes into the concrete. It was a trifle difficult for Mike Campbell, an assistant at Texas, to look all that terribly torn up for Jack Mildren since Mike's son had played for Austin Reagan, but he somehow managed to hide his pleasure. The Mildrens appreciated Campbell's position.

So Jack Mildren had a one-day reprieve, but it was the only one he would have for the next two months. Back at their home on Regent Drive in Abilene on Sunday — a small but nice development home on the new side of town — the phone calls started and the telegrams began to arrive.

The first call came from SMU coach Hayden Fry in Dallas. He just wanted to express his sorrow at Cooper losing the game. But while Hayden was at it, he managed to mention that he hoped Jack was still an SMU fan like that little redheaded, six-year-old boy he remembered so well. "You know in your heart you've always been a Mustang," Fry said to Mildren. A few hours later Jack would receive an effusive telegram from Hayden saying, among other things, that Jack was the best quarterback ever to play in the state of Texas.

The wire said in full:

JACK MILDREN

2426 REGENT ST ABILENE TEX

I SHARE YOUR GREAT DISSAPOINTMENT [sic] IN NOT WIN-
NING THE STATE CHAMPIONSHIP BUT I BECOME EXCITED
THINKING OF THE FUTURE WITH YOU AT SOUTHERN
METHODIST UNIVERSITY I AM HOPEFUL THAT THE RED
AND BLUE WILL RISE AGAIN WITH YOU LEADING THE
MUSTANGS AND RICHARD LEADING THE COUGARS STOP
CONGRATULATIONS ON A TREMENDOUS HIGH SCHOOL
CAREER STOP YOU ARE THE FINEST QUARTERBACK TO
EVERY [sic] PLAY IN THE STATE OF TEXAS STOP BEST
PERSONAL REGARDS TO YOU AND YOUR FAMILY

          HAYDEN FRY SOUTHERN METHODIST UNIVERSITY

And two others said:

JACK MILDREN

2426 REGENT ABILENE TEX

WE WOULD LOVE FOR YOU TO PLAY IN OUR NEW TEXAS
STADIUM AS A MUSTANG IN 1970

               CLINT MURCHISON JR DALLAS COWBOYS

JACK MILDREN

2426 REGENT ABILENE TEX

AS AN SMU ALUMNI, I URGE YOUR STRONG CONSIDERA-
TION OF DALLAS AND SMU AFTER COLLEGE STOP OPPOR-
TUNITY IN DALLAS IS TOPS STOP COACH FRY COACHES A

QUARTERBACK STYLE MOST CONDUCIVE TO DEVELOPMENT
AS A POTENTIAL PRO PLAYER

                    LAMAR HUNT KANSAS CITY CHIEFS

Other phone calls rapidly followed Fry's. There was Darrell Royal, who wanted to set up an official visit right away, and then several condoling assistant coaches who more or less cooled it. They just wanted to make contact. Jack granted Royal the first official visit, which would take place the following Wednesday.

Royal is a tough recruiter, because he is a direct, businesslike person who throws a challenge up to a prospect and promises nothing. This approach is designed to appeal to the competitive instinct of the athlete. Royal deals from strength. Texas was the biggest school, a good one, a pretty one and his teams had been big winners.

It took a while for Mildren to recover from Royal's presentation.

"Where do we stand, Jack?" was Royal's first question. "Is Texas in this?"

Mildren offered up several uh-uh-uhs.

"If you come to our place," said Royal, "you must know that your opportunities for success after graduation will be greater than they would be if you went anywhere else. If you plan to live in Texas you ought to attend the university. It's that simple."

Mildren, who was a most presentable and likable young man, one who had a quick handshake, a thorough knowledge of football history and the ability to converse with his elders, slowly managed to get across the idea that Texas might have too many good football players.

Royal said, "You're a competitor, Jack. Come to our place, roll up your sleeves and show 'em who's best. The challenge is there. The question is whether you're *man* enough to meet it."

Jack was hit hard by Royal. His competitive nature was aroused. He had not really ever thought that Texas would be where he would wind up, but now he did. He'd show 'em, just as Royal had challenged him to. Jack was in the perfect frame of mind to meet the easygoing entourage from TCU.

TCU's approach to recruiting over the years had always been wonderfully homey. Its basic appeal was to the small-town or country boy who wanted a howdy-type campus and who liked to whip the big guys. This sometimes had cost TCU a fine player. Like the day ex-coach Abe Martin was after Don Meredith down in Mount Vernon. He told Meredith that a beautiful thing about TCU was that he could wear Levi's and T-shirts to class, just like he did in high school. To which Meredith replied: "Coach, I been wearin' Levis and T-shirts all my life. I think I want to go someplace where they wear those pants with no belts and those loafers with those funny little tassels on 'em." Meredith, of course, went to SMU. There was a time when all of the TCU coaches chewed tobacco and pitched coins at a line outside the stadium in their spare time. A few years ago when TCU built a handsome field house with new offices for the staff, a Fort Worth columnist predicted the coaches wouldn't like it because there was no place to spit.

Jack Mildren did not hear precisely a country-boy kind of argument from Fred Taylor when the TCU coach showed in Abilene with an assistant, Allie White, and an alumnus with a private plane, oilman Dick Lowe.

"All of the schools are good," said Taylor. "You won't be disappointed with any of us. But TCU's close to your home, and we beat *Texas* last year, don't forget. We're on the winning path. We're getting close to the top, and you can take us all the way."

By now the Mildrens were not only in the dazzling social world of being entertained constantly by coaches and alumni, but Jack was regularly receiving calls and letters from great players he had heard about forever, all of them urging him to attend a different university. He got them at the rate of ten or fifteen per day from the likes of Bob Lilly, Adrian Burk, Doak Walker, Tommy Nobis, Kyle Rote, a sort of Texas Hall of Fame on long distance.

One evening the phone rang and Jack answered, fully expecting it to be another assistant coach. It wasn't at all.

"Jack," a husky voice said. "This is Johnny Unitas."

"Huh," said Jack, followed by a couple of gulps.

"I just wanted to call and put in a good word for my old friend John Bridgers at Baylor," Unitas said. "If you're as good as John says you are, then you're probably thinking about playing pro football someday."

Jack said y-yeah, h-he guessed he was, maybe.

"Well, you can't play college ball for a better coach if you want to be a pro quarterback," said Unitas. "You give Baylor some thought now, okay?"

Mildren said he would, and thanks very much for calling John, er, Mr. Unitas, er well, thankee. Thankee very much. Yes sir, Mister, uh. Thankee.

It is not easy to sell Baylor, because the Bears have not won the Southwest Conference in about a thousand years, and it is a very Baptist school, and Waco, Texas is not Beverly Hills. In fact, Waco almost has

to get two-up a side from Salado, which at least has a
dandy restaurant called the Stagecoach Inn. For a
while, however, John Unitas had Jack Mildren thinking about Baylor.

One by one, all of the head coaches got to Abilene.
Jack heard Texas Tech's J. T. King emphasize the big
money ex-Red Raider Donny Anderson had got from
the Green Bay Packers, and Larry, the father, heard
King explain how Anderson's dad was also on the
Packer payroll at $12,000 a year, if that was any kind
of inducement. J.T. said that one of the nice things
about Tech is that a boy can walk right in and see
the president. Which you sure can't do somewhere
like the University of Texas, he said. The Mildrens
listened to Houston's Bill Yeoman talk about his
unique option play and why it's better to play in the
Astrodome. They heard Rice's Bo Hagan stress education ahead of football, primarily, they suspected, because Rice has not won a conference title since 1957.

A man they listened to a little more intently than
some of the others was A&M's Gene Stallings. Like
Royal, he was speaking from strength, having lately
won the championship. He was in a hurry and he
talked to the point, except to tell a few Joe Namath
stories from his assistant coaching days at Alabama.

"If you want to learn football, there are only two
places you can consider," said Stallings, drawling

like Bear Bryant. "Alabama and Texas A&M. And I think Alabama is too far away for you. But let me say this. If you don't want to be a *one hundred percent Aggie,* don't come to our place."

While Jack was giving some thought to the rather Spartan idea of being a one hundred percent Aggie, he received what seemed like his one thousandth long-distance call of January. It came from Jerry Wampfler, a Notre Dame assistant, offering a chance to visit South Bend. Wampfler told Mildren the Fighting Irish did not go after just *anyone;* that he could be the quarterback to make everyone forget Terry Hanratty. All of the Mildrens were excited about Notre Dame phoning. It was, in a sense, the final recognition of success. Jack told the Irish he was flattered, but he truthfully wanted to stay closer to home.

Where exactly *would* Jack Mildren visit at this point? Well, he had managed to slim his choices down to about seven campuses. There were SMU, TCU, Rice and Houston, all four of which were schools where he felt he could play a lot as a sophomore. And then there were Texas, Oklahoma and Arkansas, where the competition might be greater but the chances of winning a national championship also greater. He had been to Oklahoma during the season, and Arkansas had yet to show all that much interest (although it would). He would visit the others, he thought, and hope to be persuaded, one way or another.

Normally, a potential recruit comes and goes quietly on his campus visits. He meets the coaches and also a few members of the varsity, if they aren't busy shooting snooker or sleeping. He timidly eats at the training table, and some player he may have something in common with is provided as an escort to show him a few of the prettier girls in the student union, and maybe some of the easier cabinets to jimmy open and steal test questions from. He is handed some folders, a brochure, some T-shirts and pennants. Then it's dinner and sure hope you sign up with us, Hoss.

The Mildrens were treated a little differently, not too much unlike a royal family from the Continent. In Austin, Jack was turned over to Steve Worster, the Longhorns' prized fullback. He got Jack a date, took him to a dance and showed him around. The family was then taken to dinner with Royal and his wife, Edith, other coaches and their wives, and a man named Jack Crosby, who, at the time, was Larry Mildren's boss.

It was more of the same in Houston. Jack toured the campus with Bo Burris, a former Houston standout now with the New Orleans Saints. He went to the Astrodome and saw his name flashed on the big scoreboard. Later he would receive a personal letter from Judge Roy Hofheinz.

In Fort Worth the quarterback was taken to lunch at Shady Oaks Country Club, where none other than Ben Hogan was his host. He was introduced to a lovely thing by the name of Molly Grubb, who happened to be Miss Texas at the time and a TCU student. None of this, however, made the impact on him that Dallas and SMU did.

First of all he had been getting those wires from the notable citizens, pleading with him to attend SMU. Then a group of Dallas businessmen — they were called "the millionaires" by Abilene people — made a special trip to see Jack and throw a lavish dinner at Abilene's Petroleum Club. They dwelled continually on the benefits of playing in Dallas. Big business wants you, Jack, they said.

So it was that when the Mildrens visited Dallas the first thing they saw when they arrived at the Hilton Inn, near the campus, was the marquee out front: DALLAS WELCOMES THE MILDRENS. Then, driving to the SMU campus, they saw another sign on a Tom Thumb grocery store: WELCOME TO SMU! DALLAS WELCOMES THE MILDRENS. When they got to SMU's coliseum the Mustang band, to their astonishment, was out front loudly playing the school fight song. Thereafter Jack was introduced at half time of an SMU basketball game, a party was thrown for the family at a private home and he met all sorts of Miss Teenage Dallases.

A few days later it appeared that Dallas had won the battle and that Jack had made up his mind. When SMU coach Hayden Fry phoned him Jack said, "The way things stand right now, it looks like I'll be coming to SMU."

Fry was jubilant. He said he would like to stage a massive press reception. He wanted copies of Jack's glowing statistics. He wanted to make the announcement for Sunday's papers. Then more wires began to arrive. Sign now, they said, and they came from just plain folks like Murchisons, Hunts and Merediths.

To his father, Jack paused and said, "I didn't think I was that definite. Did I mislead 'em? I'm still sort of thinking about some other schools."

And Jack did not sign.

It was at this point that Oklahoma and Arkansas, a new entry, made their big moves. Frank Broyles breezed into Abilene with his evangelistic style. No one sells anything the way Broyles sells Arkansas. He talked about his pro-type offense. He said he had hired the best quarterback coach in the country, Don Breaux from Florida State, and the best receiving coach, Richard Williamson from Alabama. He drew pass patterns incessantly, talked technical football over and over, preached the enthusiasm of the Razorback fans and got across the idea of nothing but national championships at Arkansas with Jack winning two or three Heisman trophies.

Now came Oklahoma coach Chuck Fairbanks. Didn't OU have *everything* that Jack desired in a university? It's out of state but still close enough to home, only three hundred miles. It is a campus town, Norman is, a beautiful school with some age to it. It would be like going *away* somewhere, Jack, but your folks could still see you play. And Oklahoma is winning again. You can play in the Cotton Bowl every year against Texas, don't forget, and probably go to some other bowls, too, in the postseason. You can start as a sophomore for us, Jack, and we can win a national championship at OU. You just can't do that at several other schools.

With the signing date past and Jack still not committed, it was natural that a lot of people, including some coaches, felt Mildren was holding out for improper inducements — that he was simply going to the highest bidder. Actually, a few exes from here and there had made some suggestions. Jack had been offered investments, with no cash output, of course. He could lease a new automobile at only ten dollars per month. Some splendid summer jobs had been casually mentioned. The offers were not definitive, nor were they listened to, and they were far from the reason that Jack had not signed. His was not an unusual problem for a teen-ager with a significant decision to make and parents willing to guide him, but not to decide for him. He could not make up his mind.

The talk continued. And now the family listened to all kinds of things that disturbed them. When the father left the cable TV company to go to work for American Mud, a company which sells to oil explorers, it was said that he had been fired because Jack wasn't going to Texas (the cable TV owner was a Longhorn booster) and that Oklahoma exes had fixed up the other job so they could give him a lot of business — if Jack went to OU. A newspaper ran the story that Merrill Green could join the coaching staff of whatever school Jack picked. Another paper printed the story that several schools would take the whole Cooper High backfield if Jack came. The Mildrens' postman told Jack's quiet, pleasant and bewildered mother, Mary Glynne, "If he goes to Oklahoma, I'll never root for him again." And he kept getting anti-OU wires and letters. One of them said, "How will you feel when those stupid Okies boo *The Eyes of Texas?* Another brutally said, "I is gonna be yo roommate at Oklahoma." It was signed, "Abraham Washington."

Finally Jack made up his mind. It was two months, twenty-seven official coaching visits, five hundred letters, one hundred telegrams and one hundred fifty long-distance calls later, but he made his decision. He felt sure about his choice, but he wanted to sleep on it one more night. As he slept, both Oklahoma coach Chuck Fairbanks and Arkansas coach Frank Broyles were in Abilene waiting for the word. Mildren had managed to narrow it down to those two.

The next morning Jack awakened, and his family watched as he called Frank Broyles at the Starlite Motel.

"Coach Broyles," said the quarterback. "I just wanted to let you know first that it's going to be Oklahoma."

Chuck Fairbanks made a big thing out of it, as anyone could have guessed. He called a press group together and pronounced it "a great day for Oklahoma recruiting." Jack signed the surrender papers while the family and the Oklahoma coaches and a cluster of reporters and photographers looked on.

Some other coaches made a big thing out of it, too. They all denounced the two-visit rule in the Southwest Conference, which they thought was the biggest aid Oklahoma had. His high school coach guided him to Oklahoma all the way, they said. Some schools were strung along just for the publicity, they said. And for the trips. All of this was too bad, they said, because Jack was a good kid and they wished him well.

A few months later Jack Mildren arrived at Norman in a most unusual way. There were no bands playing and no press conferences. His name was not on the marquee of a motel or even on a sign at a supermarket. No Miss Wheatfield greeted him, and no millionaires were around waiting to invite him to lunch. He was just another freshman brought in to play football, like hundreds of others across the U.S.

With some very real work ahead of him, Jack Mildren thought of only one thing. Somewhere in the past, in those giddy months of early spring, a recruiter had told him, "Once you make your decision, never look back."

He thought he would try to follow that advice now, and he decided that the world might hear of him again — and it might not. But he knew it wouldn't matter to the recruiters. Somewhere out there right now, he realized, there was another Jack Mildren, another Head Hoss, and everybody was in hot pursuit.

# 11

## One Saturday

*Orange Juice meets the Great One.*

IT was so garishly theatrical that it really should
have started at a soda fountain in a Hollywood
drugstore. Like: there were these two young college
guys named Gary and O.J., and they were sitting
there hoping to get this idea for a football show discovered by somebody big. Howard Cosell, maybe. Or
Jack Whitaker. But they kept being ignored because
it was such a tough town. There was all this competition around from Dodgers and Rams, Angels and
Lakers, Kings, Amigos and Toros, who were among
the twelve thousand professional sports teams in the
area. And then there were all of these other diver-
sions that Los Angeles just naturally offered: surfing,
sky diving, topless motorcycling, translucent mini-
skirting and teen-age protesting for the individual's
inalienable right to smoke his front lawn. Anyhow,

these two college kids, Gary Beban and O. J. Simpson, were a little despondent. They didn't even want their taco-flavored malteds. "Woe," they said. And "heck."

Suddenly one of them had an inspiration. Maybe, just maybe, he thought, they could put on their own show. Beban knew where there was this old coliseum they could use. Simpson said their schools would probably print up the tickets. Dad and Mom could be the cheerleaders. Dig out the old outfits. Heck, why not? Throw in a few of the old Morley Drury routines. Perhaps a Paul Cameron dance step. Or the Grenny Lansdell shuffle. Terrific. And look, Gary Beban has already written the title tune on a napkin: *Buckle Down, John Heisman.*

It was, of course, too Hollywood for belief. That UCLA's glamorous quarterback, Gary Beban, and USC's glamorous halfback, O. J. Simpson, could emerge in the same city, in the same conference, as the best players of 1967, was improbable enough. That they could also wind up battling for the national championship, the Rose Bowl bid and the Heisman Trophy, all on one unbearable Saturday afternoon, was strictly from the studio lots.

But there it was that Saturday, the Trojans against the Bruins before 93,000 in the Los Angeles Memorial Coliseum and millions more on ABC-TV's national telecast — a game played for more trophies, titles and prestige than any single college contest ever.

Of course, the game would have been immense, dramatic, historical, all of that, if it had matched total strangers under those same conditions. And it was equally true that almost every USC-UCLA game is worthwhile. But to bring two such dedicated enemies, two universities so close in proximity (ten miles) yet galaxies apart in image and attitude, down to so desperate an hour made the attraction all the more noteworthy.

Consider first the ironies and contrasts of the campuses. Here sat UCLA, a sprawling state institution with an enrollment of 29,000 students of varying backgrounds, colors, politics and ideals, and with generous portions of everything from hippies to Harlows, located right where, according to USC, it does not belong. UCLA is on a lovely rise called Westwood, just beneath the elegant neighborhood of Bel Air, a five-minute Mercedes ride from the dining, drinking and shopping splendors of Beverly Hills.

And over there sat USC, older by far, the smug, conservative, private school, with all of its scrubbed, predominantly white, Protestant, slow-smiling, basically upper-middle-class types. Just look where it is, laughs UCLA — practically in the middle of Watts, for God's sake. Southern Cal's campus is, in fact, flanked by rows of condemned paint stores, auto parts companies and junk shops, and only a few moments from the disenchantment of downtown L.A.

If USC could pick itself up and move, it probably would, and UCLA might be inclined to suggest Darien, Connecticut, as a suitable site, or perhaps a site under a giant old Goldwater billboard in Marin County. For a long time USC was located in a posh area of the city; only the sectors around it changed. There is always much to relish about traditions, and somehow USC's intimate red-brick buildings, its tree-lined streets and the general atmosphere within its boundaries offer more of a collegiate flavor than modern UCLA.

For the steadfast USC man, UCLA will never represent more than it was in its beginning, a preparatory facility for teachers who wanted to continue their studies elsewhere, a school unwittingly named Los Angeles State Normal, the poor school, the catchall, the school that gave us Tokyo Rose.

On the other hand, UCLA finds it difficult to be troubled these days by whatever USC thinks of it. It is too busy growing. Still pretty much of a commuter school — as is USC — it is so vast that half of the campus could protest the world's wrongdoings and the other half wouldn't know it.

As the real Gary Beban said, "We have an awful

lot of everything around here, so there's really no such thing as a sports celebrity."

There were sports heroes in earlier days, of course, particularly at USC. Over the years no university has enjoyed more all-round athletic success than Southern California, and only Notre Dame has a more treasured football past. In the 1920's and 1930's, before professional sports turned California into a world's fair of promotion, USC was just about the only thing Los Angeles citizens could take a sporting interest in. They poured into the coliseum to see Howard Jones's teams win that era's version of national championships. Players like Morley Drury, Russ Saunders, Erny Pinckert, Johnny Baker, Cotton Warburton, Grenny Lansdell, Harry Smith, Amby Schindler and Al Krueger enjoyed a celebrity status in L.A. unmatched by almost anyone of the 1960's except Sandy Koufax.

Although UCLA had its brief flurries of figures to worship, such as Kenny Washington in the 1930's and Bob Waterfield in the 1940's, it was not until the late Red Sanders went to Westwood to coach in the 1950's that the Bruins became a force the Trojans would forever have to respect. Sanders turned UCLA into a consistent national power, won a No. 1 ranking in 1954 and established his own instant list of immortals.

Being the rivals they are, the two schools have produced some athletically oriented heroes who never suited up for a game, and a wonderfully inventive group they have been. For instance, ever since a statue of an armed Trojan warrior was unveiled in 1930 at USC, its sword repeatedly has been stolen by Bruin invaders. Tommy Trojan, which is the statue's nickname, has frequently been further victimized by daubs of blue and gold paint — UCLA's colors — and by even less acceptable materials.

The nickname, Trojans, came from a sportswriter named Owen R. Bird of the *Los Angeles Times.* In a moment of rare literary achievement in 1912 he wrote of the USC track team, "They worked like Trojans." And so have the pranksters throughout the football series. There was the night that USC students slipped onto the Bruins' campus with brick and mortar and sealed up all the doors and windows of a sorority house. Two UCLA students once rented a single-engine aircraft and strafed the Trojans' campus with blue and gold paint, and two other UCLA students came over in a helicopter one year and attempted to dive-bomb Tommy Trojan with fertilizer. They missed, but the neighborhood was not an inviting place for a few hours.

A group of exceptionally depraved fun-lovers once planted dynamite in the heart of UCLA's homecoming bonfire, and when it exploded windows were shattered in Bel Air. Sometime Bel Air resident Howard Hughes obviously wasn't home that evening, or he would have bought USC and moved it to Las Vegas.

Not all of the pregame stunts have worked out, naturally. There was the time some Trojans tried to explode a smoke bomb under the UCLA yell leader's platform in the coliseum. The timing mechanism was set for 2 P.M. so that on the kickoff the Bruin cheerleaders would go up in, well, smoke. But the bomb failed. There was also the fanatic who rigged a land mine under one goal line of the coliseum and ran the detonator wire to a certain seat — his — in the rooting section. Apparently, his aim was to prevent a touchdown at all possible cost. His plot was uncovered before he was able to blast a ballcarrier into football history.

The only rational explanation for the severity of the pranks is the intensity of the division between the schools, a form of L.A. gap that in the case of this football game extended to the two head coaches, the stars and the style of play that could be expected. USC's Johnny McKay and UCLA's Tommy Prothro were as different as the campuses they represented. Both men had produced winners, had molded All-Americas, had displayed originality and had gotten a consistent effort from their players. They rated by any standard, among the best coaches in the country. But the similarities ended quite abruptly with their reputations and their statistics. As individuals, John McKay and Tommy Prothro were about as much alike as a Trojan and a bear. They differed physically, socially and instinctively, and it was easy to imagine that they might not like one another a whole lot. Respect, yes. Like? No, sir.

There were several obvious contrasts in the two men. Prothro was bigger, taller, slightly older and had been a head coach five years longer than McKay. He was quieter, more withdrawn, certainly more secretive. McKay was generally open and friendly, a wisecrack artist in his profession. It was easy to imagine Prothro as a rancher. It was just as easy to imagine McKay, a careful dresser who leaned toward sun-bleached slacks, as a golf pro. Among their colleagues, Prothro most closely resembled Alabama's Bear Bryant in drawl, manner and attitude. Quick, talkative and well organized in the contemporary, gray-flannel way, McKay was similar to Texas's Darrell Royal.

For two men totally committed to their work, they led very different lives. McKay was a little better entrenched in Los Angeles than Prothro, although Prothro was Red Sanders's top assistant in UCLA's glory days before going to Oregon State and manufacturing miracle teams, one of which featured Terry Baker, a Heisman Trophy winner. Prothro had been back as the head coach at UCLA only two full seasons, while McKay had been head coach at USC since 1960, had the security of a national championship behind him ('62), two Rose Bowl appearances and a couple of glittering upsets of Notre Dame, which he loved more than just about anything. McKay's circle of friends was a wide one, and he moved about the city with ease. He was perfectly comfortable in the presence of movie stars, and he knew several well, among them John Wayne and Bill Cosby, both of whom were big USC fans.

By comparison, Prothro was a hermit. He did not play golf, which in itself made him almost unique among football coaches, nor did he socialize much. Football was both his work and a hobby. He enjoyed staying awake for hours fiddling with various football statistics — such as rating the nation's top teams with his own mathematical formula and figuring ways to get better blocking angles off his shifting T, which was really a disguised single wing. The only other games he could tolerate were bridge and chess. Football consumed his life; he once stayed up for seventy-two consecutive hours preparing for an opponent.

Though he seldom volunteered a statement about his teams, Prothro did answer intelligent questions directly and honestly and often with a droll humor that startled the unsuspecting. Only a few days before the game, for instance, he made the comment that he had once again voted for USC as the No. 1 team in the UPI coaches' poll, but when a writer asked him why he thought the Trojans were the best team, Tommy smiled, "I didn't say they were the best team. I said I voted for them as Number One."

There was an equally distinct difference between the two players who had brought their teams to high national ranking — the halfback, Simpson, who rolled right over you, and the quarterback, Beban, who rolled around you.

For the seven and a half games of the season that Orenthal James Simpson had been whole, he had seemed to possess the finest combination of speed and power within the memory of any pro scout. He rushed for 1,238 yards in that span, and until his mishap in the Oregon game — a sprained instep that knocked him off his feet and onto crutches — he was a good bet to break the NCAA yardage record (which he would, indeed, break a year later). Not only did he crash repeatedly into stacked defenses and still wedge his way out and slice and dart for yardage, he caught passes and threw them at the least expected moments.

A mild, warm, talkative transfer from City College of San Francisco, Simpson was at first pretty bewildered by his achievements and his acclaim. He had never really been an endurance runner. Most of his two seasons at CCSF he divided his time between split end and halfback, but still he scored fifty-four touchdowns, breaking a record set by Ollie Matson.

McKay was not sure whether Simpson would be a tailback or a flanker or a split end when he recruited him. He found out quickly in spring practice. O.J. attended practice only seven days, partly because he wanted to run on the USC 440-yard relay team that set a world record of 38.6 at the NCAA Championships and partly because the coaches had learned all they needed to know.

"We wanted to see if he could take it inside," said McKay. "We ran him seven straight times in one scrimmage, and that was it. He busted people backward."

Still, O.J. never imagined that he would be asked to carry the ball as often as he had. Like thirty-eight times against Notre Dame, thirty-six against Michigan State and thirty against both Texas and Washington. "I don't get real tired," he said. "Maybe it's because I'm anticipating that on the next carry I'll break clear. I feel like I can go all the way every time, mainly because we've got such a good line."

McKay felt that Simpson, who was 6′ 1″ and weighed 202, was the fastest runner for his size who ever played the game. His 9.4 clocking in the 100-yard dash was an often-mentioned figure, but it was not as impressive as his 4.5 at 40 yards in football shoes. USC's other speedster, Earl the Pearl McCullouch, had done a 4.4, but he was 35 pounds lighter and one of the world s fastest high hurdlers. The two took turns beating each other informally in a "football 100," and Simpson swapped victories with Mc-Cullouch in the indoor 60-yard dash.

Simpson, who had married his high school sweetheart and lived in an apartment three blocks from the USC campus, had attracted almost as much attention with his nickname — Orange Juice — as he had with his statistics. He did not get the name in southern California. He had it in San Francisco, and he was not sure, but he believed it came from some television commercial about orange juice. (His real name, Orenthal, was given him by an aunt, who, he wryly noted, used things like Stewart and James when the time came to name her own children.)

Coaches, scouts and writers tried to figure out all season who it was Simpson's running style reminded them of. He exhibited the raw burst of speed that Mel Renfro had in college and some of the deceptive moves of Gale Sayers. But he also slammed in there and broke tackles like Jim Brown. Given daylight, he slid through with the nifty balance of Jon Arnett.

As deft as any move Simpson ever made was the one Southern California used to land him and keep him hooked for an extra year at City College of San Francisco when O.J. truly wanted to leave. Simpson was born and grew up in San Francisco, where his father was a custodian for the Federal Reserve Bank. When he graduated from Galileo High School, which also turned loose such athletic figures as Joe DiMaggio, Hank Luisetti and Lawson Little, his transcript was not the kind that had Harvard seeking out his father at the Federal Reserve. O.J. entered City College of San Francisco in the hope of making good enough grades to get into a major college eventually, probably California. But as soon as he put on a football suit, other schools became interested, among them USC.

"When I decided I wanted to go to USC after my first year in City College, I still did not have the grades," said Simpson. "So I had to make a big decision. Arizona State and Utah sounded good to me because I could go to either one and play ball right away. I almost enrolled at Arizona State, but the

USC coaches talked me into holding out for the big time. That is the luckiest thing that ever happened to me, even if I did have to spend another year going to junior college."

By leaving the San Francisco area to go to school down south, Simpson was following at least one pair of notable footsteps: Gary Beban's. "Why, Beban has been my idol," said Simpson. "Seriously. It's funny. He's from my part of the state, and I followed him closely for two years while I was in junior college. I watched him play on television, and in the Rose Bowl and all. He's great, man. It sure seems strange to be on a team now that wants to beat him."

Gary Beban, the UCLA answer to Orange Juice, was one of those athletes who did things with infuriating ease. He passed with classic form, and he ran gracefully, almost in slow motion except that he managed to turn the corners and slide through. When his passes were in the air, the ball somehow looked longer, and the spiral was perfect, as if Beban had figured out exactly how many rotations it should make. His ball handling was superb, his faking even better. But above everything else, Beban had poise.

Said a scout: "He is about the most self-assured player I've ever seen. He knows exactly what he is going to do, and he will spot things out there, file them away mentally and use them on you later. You don't judge Beban on how much he does, not on his statistics. He beats you with the 'when' he does something. Invariably it's at the perfect time."

Prothro often said that Beban could beat you with a run, pass, fake or call, and that his ability to change plays at the scrimmage line was perhaps his finest asset. A familiar sight for three seasons was Beban behind the center, shifting his backs, then checking, raising his head to survey the defense and shouting another play that unfolded perfectly. In the clutch.

"There's something about the way he manages things out there that gives everyone confidence," said fullback Rick Purdy. "You just know whatever he calls is right."

Beban came about as close to being the cinemascopic ideal of a college star as anyone could. It was said that he resembled a young Marlon Brando, but he was not so roughhewn as that. Personable and natural, quick-smiling and polite, he possessed, at twenty-one, a maturity not found in all that many undergraduates. A history major, he would graduate on schedule with fairly decent grades.

For a football hero who was about to be proclaimed an All-America, and possibly the Heisman Trophy winner as well — in fact, for one who had been the class quarterback of the nation for three straight seasons and had come to be known as the Great One — Beban lived like a freshman. He shared an off-campus apartment with Larry Slagle, a tackle; John Erquiaga, a center; and Steve Stanley, a reserve fullback. The floors were reasonably clean, the records in findable condition and all of the knobs on the TV set were intact. Two large photographs were on the wall — the touchdown catches that Beban's receivers, Kurt Altenberg and Dick Witcher, made in the comeback win over USC in 1965. Beban insisted he was the farthest thing from a big man on the UCLA campus, or a social lion. He dated irregularly, had not been on the Sunset Strip since beards began to grow and his idea of a good time was either loafing around the apartment talking football with his teammates or inviting dates over and showing a film of a game UCLA won.

"I suppose I'm rather ordinary," Beban said. Uh, huh. And O. J. Simpson was ordinary too.

But of all the differences between USC and UCLA as their big Saturday neared, the one that mattered the most was how the two teams played football. Thanks to their coaches, they had different approaches to the game.

McKay's Trojans were basically offensive-minded, though they surely played good defense. The Trojans were attackers. They moved the ball from a flamboy-

ant, well-conceived I formation that McKay himself
had refined to include motion, shifting and zone-
wrecking passes. It was the prettiest offense in the
land, and lots of smart people were trying to copy it.
Prothro's Bruins were defensive fanatics. They were
fast and outlandishly aggressive. Like Alabama,
Texas, Tennessee, Arkansas, all consistently provok-
ing defensive teams, UCLA swarmed on its foe. It
stunted and squirmed, hit and slid, penetrated and
scrambled and forced mistakes. Offensively, UCLA
was cool, balanced and capable of striking fast.

Since early in the season when USC and UCLA
attained their top-level rankings in the national polls,
trying to rate their strengths and deficiencies had
been a parlor game. You gave USC a point for
offense, UCLA a point for defense. You gave USC
strength, but UCLA got quickness. USC had a better
blocking line, but UCLA had a better pursuing defense. UCLA had the best passing, but USC had the
best receiving. The kicking was even, the coaching
was even, and there was no home-field advantage. At
first it seemed that USC had struggled through a far
more difficult schedule, beating Texas, Michigan
State and Notre Dame and losing only to that champion of all upset teams, Oregon State, while UCLA
had defeated only Tennessee among the respectable
powers. It then occurred to analysts that the Vols

might be a better team than any USC had played. On the other hand, UCLA suffered two terribly narrow escapes against weaker teams — Penn State and Stanford — that easily might have defeated the Bruins and tied Oregon State.

"We've been good when we had to," Prothro said.

And McKay replied, "We've had to be good."

For any big football game, there are more so-called intangibles than there are long-lost chums who want tickets. Intangibles involve emotion, character, voodoo, tradition and intuition. And as far as emotion went, UCLA's players were most likely to look as if they had reached the higher, more frenzied peak, but that was how the Bruins usually looked and how Prothro encouraged them to look. USC would be just as high for the day, but the Trojans would look a lot calmer about things, a lot more workmanlike.

So who would win? A day before the game, a man who should be able to judge the situation well, John McKay himself, went to a blackboard and evaluated the two teams, player by player. He had a point grading system for this, and when he was through adding point by point, he totaled the figures for each team. Just like in the Hollywood script, they came out exactly equal. When that happened, McKay stepped back from the blackboard and made the

least newsworthy comment of the most exciting football season Los Angeles had ever known:

"It's going to be a helluva game," he said.

And here is the way it was in that college football
game for the championship of the earth, Saturn,
Pluto and Los Angeles: UCLA's Gary Beban slowly
developed a rib cage that looked like an abstract
painting in purples and pinks, and USC's O. J. Simpson had a bandaged foot that looked like it belonged
in a museum of natural history, but they kept getting
up from these knockout blows, gasping, coming back,
and doing all of their outrageously heroic things. So,
do you know what?

In the end, the difference was that this guy with a
name like a Russian poet, Zenon Andrusyshyn,
couldn't place-kick the ball over this other guy with
a name like the president of the Van Nuys Jaycees —
Bill Hayhoe. Andrusyshyn would try to side-boot a
field goal or extra point for UCLA, and Hayhoe, who
happened to be 6′ 8″, would rise up. The ball would
go splat, plink or karang. The last time Hayhoe did
it, he tipped the leather just enough to make the
Bruins fail on a precious conversion, and USC got
away with a 21–20 victory in a spectacle that will be
remembered for ages, or at least as long as German-
born, Ukrainian, Canadian-bred soccer-style kickers
play the game.

Of course, it was not exactly fair to insinuate that Zenon Andrusyshyn, the German-Ukrainian-Canadian, was the goat of the whole desperate afternoon. Though only a sophomore, he was a splendid kicker who boomed punts into the California heavens all day, and it appeared that if the ball were given time to rise, he was capable of place-kicking one more than sixty yards. Rather, it was more accurate to give credit to USC's John McKay for one of those little coaching touches that sometimes supplies a subtle edge. This time it proved to be a subtle edge that gave McKay the most important game of his life.

"We knew he kicked it low, so we just put the tallest guy we had in there on defense," said McKay later, in what may have been the happiest dressing room since showers were invented. "We told the kids it wasn't so important that they bust through and make him rush the kicks as it was just getting to the scrimmage line and raising their arms high."

In his wry, twinkling way, McKay then lit a cigar and said, "I call that brilliant coaching."

Everything about the day was brilliant, of course — as more than 90,000 limp souls in the Los Angeles Memorial Coliseum certainly noted, and as millions of others watching on national television

must have, too. Led by those folklore characters,
Gary Beban and O. J. Simpson, both teams played
extremely well, considering the slightly barbaric circumstances. That both squads and staffs went into
the gnawing pressure of this kind of Saturday with
such poise was unique enough. But that they also
managed to litter the premises with so much brilliant
play was downright against the rules for games of
the century, era, decade, year (choose one). There
can only be one reason why the Trojans and Bruins
responded so well to the occasion, and it was that
they were, quite simply, the two best teams in the
U.S. that season.

Although neither O.J. or Beban was 100 percent
perfect physically, both were superb in clutch after
clutch. While he practically had to crawl to the
sideline no less than five times to regain his breath
because of his injured ribs, Beban whirled the Bruins
to three touchdowns, passing for more than three
hundred yards, giving his team a 7–0 lead in the first
quarter, a 14–14 tie in the third and a 20–14 lead in
the fourth.

Meanwhile, Simpson, his right foot throbbing inside a shoe with a special sponge cover, wearily
hobbled away from piles of brutal tacklers and
eventually managed to race for a total of 177 yards,

including the touchdowns that put the Trojans ahead 14–7 and finally 21–20.

Had the Heisman Trophy award, therefore, really been decided by a couple of young men named Zenon Andrusyshyn and Bill Hayhoe? As Jim Murray of the *Los Angeles Times* said, "They should send the Heisman out here with two straws."

McKay and Prothro honed their teams quite differently for the big one. The Bruins worked shorter hours, for one thing. Zip, zip, zip. It was as if Prothro was trying to conserve their energy. On the last warmup day, Friday, his team was out only seven minutes in contrast to USC's hour and a half. Across town, the Trojans ran more. Lots of wind sprints at what McKay called "party time," which was a sort of postpractice session. The defense especially ran more than normal, and it was worth noting that USC's defense was fresher at the end of the game. All of those Trojans who were chasing, and catching, Gary Beban there at the finish — ends Tim Rossovich and Jim Gunn, who was in action despite torn ligaments suffered earlier in the day, tackle Willard Scott, linebacker Adrian Young and halfback Pat Cashman — looked capable of playing another two quarters.

It was actually more necessary for USC to win the game than UCLA. Prothro had beaten McKay for the last two years, for one thing. Not only that, a feeling had emerged in the minds of many, much to McKay's anger, that Prothro had won with guile, wisdom and genius rather than athletes.

"Well," said McKay sharply one day, "we pushed 'em all over the field in 1965, but we fumbled on their one, seven and seventeen. I guess he planned that."

Anyhow, McKay was grim. Uncharacteristically grim. And USC, the team that is normally loose, was grim and quiet, right up to an hour before the start. The Trojans looked tense enough to fumble at least ten times, but O. J. Simpson argued differently.

"We're just mad," he said.

Nor was UCLA in the emotional frenzy that had been its most commonly displayed trait. The Bruins were quiet, too, concentrating. Gary Beban was told that O.J. said USC was mad, and Gary, Mister Cool, said, "Anger doesn't win football games."

For almost the first twenty minutes it looked as if UCLA was the only team in the coliseum. The Bruins were a lot quicker in the line, niftier in execution, more confident in their game plan, and more inventive in their attack. Beban had thrown the first of sixteen completions to his left end, Dave Nuttall, who would catch seven, and he had gotten eleven big yards on a keeper, and he had led the interference for Greg Jones's blasting 12-yard touchdown run, which put UCLA out front. At the same time, the Trojans had not been able to move. In five possessions they had not scratched out a first down. On his first ten carries, even behind an occasional and surprising eight-man line that McKay thought would unsettle Prothro, O. J. Simpson had gained only eleven measly yards. He had come no closer to breaking clear than Andy Williams, who was there to sing at half time.

The situation looked normal; Prothro had McKay's number, just as everyone had been saying at The Daisy, The Factory, La Scala and Stefanino's before diverting conversation back to who got which part in what TV series. It was normal except for one thing: USC did not have any yards or first downs, but it had seven points.

On the last play of the first quarter, just as it looked like Beban was cranking up the Bruins again, the UCLA quarterback threw a pass at midfield into the wide left flat. The receiver was open, as Bruin receivers were all day, but the ball hung. It may have hung because Beban's side, injured in the Washington game the previous week, prevented him from slinging the ball hard when he had to. It may have hung because he misjudged the risk of an interception. Whatever the reason, USC's Pat Cashman saw it coming. He darted in front of Greg Jones, leaped and took the ball with nothing but fifty-five yards of beautiful, unpopulated coliseum turf before him.

"I called the play," Prothro drawled later on. "It's a new one. He's supposed to roll one direction, turn and throw blind, hoping no defender's there. It's a stupid play. I'll never use it again."

While Pat Cashman's interception perked up the USC rooters — hundreds of whom, like UCLA's, had been in the stands since dawn to get good seats — it did not seem at the time to be all that important; it might hold down the score, maybe. Sure enough, after a wiggly, forty-two-yard punt return by UCLA's Mark Gustafson, the Bruins were quickly threatening again, with a first down on the 15.

But now a series of strange things happened that changed the game for the rest of the day. In three plays the Bruins got nowhere, and on the third one Beban got the first of the deadly blows in the ribs — this one courtesy of Pat Cashman — which would send him writhing toward the sideline. Andrusyshyn came in and missed a field goal from the 20. The kick was not one of those molested by Bill Hayhoe; Zenon simply side-winded it off to the left. And on USC's first play from its own 20, the game suddenly had another offensive team. Earl the Pearl McCullouch started it by streaking down the sideline off a daring reverse for fifty-two yards. McCullouch then caught a thirteen-yard pass. And now Simpson was warmed up. From thirteen yards out, O.J. burst over guard for the touchdown — one that was especially vital, for it proved to the USC offense that it could move the ball.

Still, if UCLA was impressed it did not act it. The Bruins took the kickoff amid the most noise since D-day, and Beban promptly threw a forty-eight-yard pass to Nuttall. It was first down on the Trojan 15 again. But, just like the time before, USC's defense got riled. Beban was smacked by everybody but Southern California President Norman Topping, one of nine losses he would suffer, and he had to retreat to the bench again. In came Andrusyshyn for the first of two field-goal tries that Bill Hayhoe would block.

As had been said so many times about Beban, he learns from mistakes. He could hardly wait for the second half to start to take advantage of Pat Cashman, who had intercepted him and who had buried his red USC headgear into Beban's lung. With only two minutes gone in the third quarter, Beban laid a perfect 47-yard pass into the hands of halfback George Farmer for the tying touchdown.

"Cashman had been waiting for another of those flat passes, so we sent Farmer straight down, right

past him," said Gary afterward. "It balanced out.
Cashman's interception was really responsible for
our second touchdown." Between this score and the
one that put UCLA ahead early in the fourth
quarter, Prothro's team blew another excellent opportunity. The combination of a poor punt by USC's
Rikki Aldridge, who redeemed himself for this and
all other misdeeds of a lifetime by ultimately kicking
the game-winning conversion, and a Beban pass put
UCLA on the Trojan 17. It was there that Hayhoe, a
junior from Van Nuys who weighed 254 along with
his 6′ 8″, lumbered through to drop Beban for a
whopping loss, and two plays later he blocked another field-goal attempt by the Ukrainian.

"Those things somehow weren't as discouraging
then as they are now," said Beban later as he wandered around in the USC locker room, sipping a
canned Coke, smiling and congratulating the Trojans.
"We knew we would score again."

They did. Beban hit four passes in a brisk seven-
play drive covering sixty-five yards, the last one
going to Nuttall for twenty yards and the touchdown
that made it 20–14 with only eleven minutes remaining. Andrusyshyn missed the point because Hayhoe
had gotten a finger on it, and while it occurred to
everybody in the Western world that this could be a
pretty unfortunate point to miss, UCLA still looked

like the better team. The Trojans had not seriously threatened. Junior Steve Sogge had given way to senior Toby Page at quarterback, and it was no Los Angeles secret that John McKay's wife Corky was a better passer than Page. Nor had O.J. really busted loose.

But now it was time for Simpson to get back in the Heisman derby, thanks to a thing called 23-Blast. UCLA's tough tacklers had been kindly helping O.J. back up on his feet all day, a fine sporting gesture with the subtle design of keeping Simpson from resting. And at last it was time for O.J. to knock them down. And out.

It was third down at his own 36 when Toby Page saw UCLA's linebacker move out, anticipating the play Page had called in the huddle. Page checked signals and called another play at the line. It was 23-Blast. As it unfolded, it looked like a five-yard gain. Guard Steve Lehmer and tackle Mike Taylor cleared O.J. through the hole. Then Simpson veered out toward the left sideline. Oh, well, a fifteen-yard gain and a first down. But end Ron Drake screened off UCLA's halfback, and the safety sucked over, and, hey, what's this? O.J. angled back to the middle, to his right, and a great glob of daylight became visible. And then he was running like the 9.4 sprinter he is, despite that sore foot and that funny shoe, and there was not anybody down there for the rest of the sixty-four yards who was about to catch him.

Of the remarkable 1,415 yards Simpson gained that season, those sixty-four were the most impressive of all, for they came after two hours of the toughest punishment he had endured — and they stretched all the way to Number One.

About an hour and a half after the game, down in the USC dressing room, which had finally emptied and grown as quiet as it had been before the kickoff, a brief scene was enacted that served as a fitting epilogue. Dressed now, blazers on, hair combed, refreshed, Gary Beban and O. J. Simpson met, looking like two young men anticipating a fraternity council meeting.

"Gary, you're the greatest," said O.J. "It's too bad one of us had to lose."

"O.J., you're the best," said Beban. "Go get 'em in the Rose Bowl."

O.J. grinned. Presently, he ambled down the hall, through a door and up a walkway to an exit gate where clusters of USC fans were still gathered. It was roughly, oh, about sixty-four yards.

# 12

## It's Just an Old Fordham Halfback

*But it's the Heisman Trophy and everybody
wants it.*

**H**E has never had a nickname such as Oscar or
Emmy, which is probably just an oversight of
the years, like some of the Sam Baughs and Jim
Browns who have not won him. He is only eighteen
inches tall. He weighs only fifty pounds. And he costs
only $252. He is, in fact, just an old Fordham half-
back, a dark brown hunk of sculpture running and
stiff-arming across a slab of ebony — and perhaps a
bit ill-proportioned at that, seeing as how his head
seems overly large, his shoulders are narrow, and his
legs are short. For all of this, however, few relics
that we know of have created more melodrama in
college football than the Heisman Memorial Trophy,
an award that is supposed to go to the outstanding

player in the United States every year, and sometimes does.

There have been those years, to be sure, when a
single player was so magnificent week after week
that the selection of the Heisman winner was the
worst-kept secret in America. More often, though, it
came down to which campus had put forth the
biggest effort, in terms of publicity and ballyhoo, on
behalf of its treasured ball-carrier. So it has seemed,
at least.

The battle for the Heisman begins to be waged
early in the season by all of the campus publicity
directors and the provincial writers and broadcasters
who loiter around the stars. Exactly 1,371 newsmen
are eligible to vote on the award annually, but it is a
rather unfortunate thing that the Heisman committee has trouble keeping the list up to date. An awful
lot of deceased journalists have received ballots, and
an even greater number receive them when they
have moved on to other pursuits and haven't seen a
college game in years.

I found, for example, that I used to get a Heisman
ballot every two or three years even though I was
seeing a game every Saturday, and usually a game
involving a serious candidate. At the same time, I
have known thoroughbred racing writers and news-

papermen who covered bowling and stock car racing who never failed to get a ballot. I have the nagging suspicion that a larger number of late-night disc jockeys receive ballots than any collection of hard-core football writers.

Nonetheless, the war is taken in bitter seriousness.

Very early each season one begins to hear game announcers on the radio huckstering for their home-town heroes.

"Tulane comes out of the huddle," an announcer will say, "and there's big Jock McStrap, our great right tackle, standing down there looking pretty mean. Boy, does he swallow up a ball carrier! He's going for the Heisman, you know."

Then the color man is chimed in with the play-by-play genius and we hear the following:

"During this time out, Ray, let's just take a minute or two to chat about big Jock McStrap. You've played the game, Ray, and been around it a long time, as all of our good fans know. Have you *ever* seen a better all-around football player than big Jock?"

"Well, there've been a lot of great ones, Fred, but to answer your question as honestly as I know how — I haven't."

"He's got it all, hasn't he?"

"Well, the thing about Jock is, he's not just big,

he's mobile. And he's not just fast, he's alert. And he's not just tough, he's got instinct. And he's not just tall, he's rangy. And he's not just ——"

"What about that *grade* average?"

"Well, that's right. You see a lot of kids play this game and fall down in the classroom. But they tell me big Jock's carrying a three point oh, and you never can underestimate intelligence in any walk of life, I like to say."

"We certainly know he comes from good football stock, don't we?"

"Well, that's another thing, Fred. His father used to be president of this great university, as you know. His uncle, of course, is on the board of trustees. His mother was the first lady airline pilot. I'll tell you. I like thoroughbreds. I like to say you can't underestim ——"

"Not a bad discus thrower, either, by the way."

"Well, there's something else. Arm strength and balance. Which reminds me of the day the Rock and I were ——"

"Pretty good catcher on the baseball team last spring."

"Well, it's those hands of his, of course, as I've mentioned on other broadcasts, and those strong shoulders and ——"

"I don't suppose, Ray, that we can mention it too

often about big Jock's fondness for the fine arts. Rare to find a kid as ferocious on the football field who finds time to paint and play the violin and write poetry, wouldn't you say?"

"Well, you think about how he combines all this with his interest in campus politics and boys clubs and working in the ghettos, it's ——"

"You know, Ray, I was down on the field chatting with Jock just before the kickoff today and I asked him about the Heisman Trophy and how he honestly felt about all of the publicity he's getting. I don't suppose I'll be talking out of school, so to speak, to repeat what he told me here on the air. He said, 'Fred, it's an honor that every college football player would like to win, but I'll be truthful with you. If I were fortunate enough to be awarded that great trophy, I'd consider it a *team* award.' I think that says quite a lot for Jock McStrap, Ray."

"Well, you see, you're talking about character now. I ——"

"Of course, last week, Ray, when my wife Nancy and I were having dinner with Jock and his family before the Kansas State game, the game where he made those thirty-seven unassisted tackles, I recall asking him how he felt about having to play a big game like that on two bandaged knees, and he said, 'Fred, when I go on the field with this bunch of great guys, I don't feel anything but pride.' I think that says something else about Jock McStrap, Ray."

"Well, there again, pride is somethi——"

"I see time's back in, Ray, and we've got a ball game on our hands. I see big Jock down there on all fours waiting to meet the Tulane charge and, heh, heh, *sort out* another ball carrier. We'll be right back with play-by-play action after this message from one of our sponsors."

Various wire service writers have unfortunately committed the same kind of crimes, having fallen under the influence of publicity men who spoon-feed them alibis and exaggerated statistics. As in Missouri zonked Oklahoma four million to nothing, folks, but by golly the Sooners' Steve Owens got his usual one hundred yards rushing.

No player has ever won the Heisman twice, of course. But there have been a few who came close and, as a matter of fact, weren't all that undeserving. O. J. Simpson was probably the best player in the country in both 1967 and 1968 but he couldn't outpoll Gary Beban, a senior, in '67. Doak Walker in 1947 and 1948, Frank Sinkwich in 1941 and 1942 and Tom Harmon in 1939 and 1940 were other stars who might easily have been double winners.

Which brings up the fact that the voters lean toward seniors. Only four juniors ever succeeded, they being Doc Blanchard, Doak Walker, Vic Janowicz and Roger Staubach.

The voters not only are partial to seniors, they seem to prefer talent from the Midwest and quarterbacks. A total of fourteen players from the Midwest have been so honored (eight from the Big Ten and six from Notre Dame). And a total of eighteen quarterbacks have won it. Thus, a senior quarterback from the Midwest is not the worst thing to be if you also have some talent, although none of this did much good for a couple of strong candidates from Purdue — Bob Griese and Mike Phipps. Each was led to believe he had it sacked, having received a phone call from someone connected with the Heisman telling him to be available for a press conference at noon on the appointed day of announcement, but the calls did not come. Mike Garrett and Steve Owens, a couple of workhorse runners, outpolled them.

It helps to play on a winning team, as you might guess. All but one Heisman winner has been a member of a team which won more games than it lost, and sixteen of them have played on a team which captured some kind of national championship. Notre Dame's Paul Hornung is the one loser who sneaked in on one of the great publicity coups of our age. More about that later. First, here is a list of the winners and the well-known losers of the same years:

| | THE HEISMAN WINNERS | SOME NOTABLE LOSERS |
|---|---|---|
| *1935* | *Jay Berwanger,* Chicago | *Sam Baugh,* TCU |
| *1936* | *Larry Kelley,* Yale | *Ace Parker,* Duke |
| *1937* | *Clint Frank,* Yale | *Whizzer White,* Colorado |
| *1938* | *Davey O'Brien,* TCU | *Marshall Goldberg,* Pitt |
| *1939* | *Nile Kinnick,* Iowa | *John Kimbrough,* Texas A&M |
| *1940* | *Tom Harmon,* Michigan | *Frankie Albert,* Stanford |
| *1941* | *Bruce Smith,* Minnesota | *Bill Dudley,* Virginia |
| *1942* | *Frank Sinkwich,* Georgia | *Glenn Dobbs,* Tulsa |
| *1943* | *Angelo Bertelli,* Notre Dame | *Creighton Miller,* Notre Dame |
| *1944* | *Les Horvath,* Ohio State | *Bob Fenimore,* Oklahoma A&M |
| *1945* | *Doc Blanchard,* Army | *Harry Gilmer,* Alabama |
| *1946* | *Glenn Davis,* Army | *Charley Trippi,* Georgia |
| *1947* | *Johnny Lujack,* Notre Dame | *Bobby Layne,* Texas |
| *1948* | *Doak Walker,* SMU | *Charley Justice,* North Carolina |
| *1949* | *Leon Hart,* Notre Dame | *Eddie LeBaron,* College of Pacific |
| *1950* | *Vic Janowicz,* Ohio State | *Kyle Rote,* SMU |
| *1951* | *Dick Kazmier,* Princeton | *Babe Parilli,* Kentucky |

| | THE HEISMAN WINNERS | SOME NOTABLE LOSERS |
|---|---|---|
| 1952 | Billy Vessels, Oklahoma | Leon Hardeman, Georgia Tech |
| 1953 | John Lattner, Notre Dame | Paul Cameron, UCLA |
| 1954 | Alan Ameche, Wisconsin | Dicky Moegle, Rice |
| 1955 | Howard Cassady, Ohio State | Jim Swink, TCU |
| 1956 | Paul Hornung, Notre Dame | Jim Brown, Syracuse |
| 1957 | John David Crow, Texas A&M | Clendon Thomas, Oklahoma |
| 1958 | Pete Dawkins, Army | Randy Duncan, Iowa |
| 1959 | Billy Cannon, LSU | Don Meredith, SMU |
| 1960 | Joe Bellino, Navy | Bill Kilmer, UCLA |
| 1961 | Ernie Davis, Syracuse | James Saxton, Texas |
| 1962 | Terry Baker, Oregon State | Jerry Stovall, LSU |
| 1963 | Roger Staubach, Navy | Gale Sayers, Kansas |
| 1964 | John Huarte, Notre Dame | Joe Namath, Alabama |
| 1965 | Mike Garrett, USC | Bob Griese, Purdue |
| 1966 | Steve Spurrier, Florida | Mel Farr, UCLA |
| 1967 | Gary Beban, UCLA | Terry Hanratty, Notre Dame |
| 1968 | O. J. Simpson, USC | Leroy Keyes, Purdue |
| 1969 | Steve Owens, Oklahoma | Mike Phipps, Purdue |

The Heisman is presented by the Downtown Athletic Club of New York and named for John W. Heisman, who was a coach in ancient days whose lasting contribution to the game — before the trophy — was the invention of the center snap. No one knows why or how all of this glory came to the award. It wasn't due to John W.'s coaching record at Auburn, Clemson, Georgia Tech, Penn, Washington and Jefferson and Rice. And in no way could it be due to the influence of the club itself. The club is a thirty-five-story building in lower Manhattan which rattles and creaks with four thousand members, four hundred fifty employees, four bowling alleys, six squash courts, a gym, a swimming pool, and is absolutely unheard of and unthought about by non-members between Heisman award dinners.

Possibly, it was because the Heisman came first, in 1935, two years ahead of a couple of other individual awards, the Camp and Maxwell trophies. Also, it could have something to do with being based in New York City amid all of the glitter that some people believe to be there. As far back as 1938, I know, it was a fun thing to accompany your Heisman winner to the big town and do a lot of whooping. When TCU's Davey O'Brien was the recipient that year, a trainload of rich Texans came along with him, rented a city fire engine, put on their biggest Stetsons, and rode up and down the avenues, waving and hollering at what must have been a truly astonished group of taxi drivers and doormen.

Still in this spirit, the Heisman winner is toasted and paraded all around midtown during his stay, during which time he is also TV'd and radio'd and newspapered, all of it being a part of how the New York press rediscovers college football every December.

Technically the trophy, which *was* conceived by a sculptor (Frank Eliscu) who *did* use a Fordham halfback for a model, is awarded to the player piling up the most points in the vote, a national vote, supposedly. However, the number of votes per section of the country depends on the number of accredited universities and colleges in that area, which *does* give the East and Midwest an edge.

The weight that publicity men have had on the selection is most likely exaggerated. But this doesn't keep the campus flacks from thinking they sometimes win for their boys. The most notable jobs seem to have been done at Notre Dame, naturally.

Among those feats are these: Leon Hart becoming only the second lineman ever to win, Angelo Bertelli taking the trophy in 1943 when he played only five games (he got called to duty by the Marines at midseason), and John Huarte, a total unknown at the season's beginning, winning over such supercandidates in 1964 as Joe Namath, Tucker Frederickson, Gale Sayers, Craig Morton, Jerry Rhome and Dick Butkus.

But the best of all was Paul Hornung. He won over perhaps more supercandidates than Huarte as the Notre Dame mystique was utterly baffling. Here, around the country, were such stalwarts as Jim Brown at Syracuse, Johnny Majors at Tennessee, Tommy McDonald and Jerry Tubbs at Oklahoma (which also happened to be in the midst of Bud Wilkinson's forty-seven-game win streak), and Jim Swink and Del Shofner and John Crow down in the Southwest. Meanwhile, Hornung's Notre Dame team was getting clobbered: 0–40 by Oklahoma, 14–47 by Michigan State, 7–33 by Navy and 8–48 by Iowa. It finished with a dazzling 2–8 record.

But Hornung had Notre Dame and Charlie Callahan going for him.

Callahan was the publicity man in South Bend then, and he knew where the power was. Big cities. Radio. Television. Syndicated columnists. Notre Dame was terrible, he admitted, but, gee, this Hornung was great, week after week, fighting all the odds. Golden Boy. All that.

In later years, Charlie liked to reminisce about his conquest like a prize-fight manager. "That was the year Harold Keith at Oklahoma made the mistake of trying to sell an interior lineman — Tubbs. He didn't switch his emphasis to McDonald until mid-season, but it was too late."

Charlie explained, "The East went for Jim Brown, the South for Majors, Tubbs, McDonald, Swink and all of those cut each other up. I had the Midwest to myself, and enough pieces of other sections to skim by."

Callahan was so proud of the victory that he sent for Hornung in class to tell him personally. But as Paul walked across the South Bend campus, past the golden dome and Moses, and headed toward Charlie's small cluttered office, the publicity man placed a long distance call to Paul's mother in Louisville, Kentucky, and he had her waiting on the phone when Hornung strolled in, wondering what Callahan wanted.

Charlie just sat there without looking up, casually pretending to be sorting through the debris on his desk. He handed the receiver to Hornung and mumbled something.

"Here," Callahan said. "Tell your mother you just won the Heisman."

That is my second favorite Heisman story. My favorite concerns Les Horvath, the Ohio State tailback who won the award on the Buckeyes' "civilian" team of 1944. True or not, it's a banquet-saver.

It seems that Horvath and his wife moved out to Los Angeles in about 1947, soon after World War II, in any case, and Horvath's wife noticed this ugly statue being unpacked and placed on the living room mantel.

"What's that thing?" she asked. "Out. Get it out of here."

Horvath explained that it was among his most prized possessions. He explained what it was. What he had done a few years before to win it. Couldn't he just leave it there for the time being? If she really disapproved, he would move it to another room. Fine.

A couple of nights later the Horvaths happened to have dinner at the home of the Tom Harmons, and Horvath's wife noticed that a Heisman Trophy adorned Harmon's mantel. And two nights later they happened to have dinner with the Glenn Davises, and Horvath's wife noticed that another Heisman Trophy had adorned that mantel as well.

Driving home that evening she turned to Les and said:

"You know that thing you want to keep in the living room? I wish you would tell me what's so special about it? Everybody we *know* has one."

# 13

## Woody

*Hayes, of course, and Middle America and winning.*

*Keep cool, Baby.*
*And run those fat tackles to death.*

**T**HESE were the words that would stay with Woody Hayes out there in Middle America. He would always like to quote others, poets, generals and admirals, applying the words to football. And to his enemies, which were many, he would always seem a little like the way Winston Churchill described General Montgomery: "Indomitable in defeat, insufferable in victory." That was sure Woody. But it would be *his* words that football would remember. "Being cold, like being determined to win, is just a state of mind," he would say, walking into a blizzard in his short sleeves. And, boy, would

Woody's Ohio State Buckeyes run those fat tackles every Saturday.

Ohio State is an enormous arrangement of gray buildings and smokestacks along the Olentangy River out in Columbus, Ohio. One thinks of it as nearly always being cold and overcast around Ohio State. And Columbus has never been the best of towns to get stranded in. There might be a few bars connected with motels where you could find a piano player and some friendly souls willing to take off their mackinaws and sing one or two Big Ten fight songs. Downtown there was a belly dancer. No, the fun in Columbus only occurred on Saturdays in the fall when Woody's Buckeyes lumbered into this great gray edifice of a stadium that held over 80,000.

The Buckeyes would go in there wearing their scarlet and gray with nothing but linemen and full-backs — and perhaps an occasional Howard Cassady — and they would run everybody's fat tackles right back to Ann Arbor or Evanston or Bloomington or Madison, any of those other thrilling metropolises of the Big Ten. They would do it with an attack that the world would label "three yards and a cloud of dust," but this would not matter to Woody Hayes.

"Winning," he would say, "takes care of everything."

Other teams might have stars with glamorous

names like Pistol Pete or Roger the Dodger or The Golden Boy, but Woody stuck with Middle America. He had big, trim, square-jawed fellows named Jim and Bob — Jim Parker and Jim Marshall and Jim Davidson, and Bob White and Bob Ferguson.

Every week Ohio State would fill up with over 80,000 worshippers, and every week the highlight of the game would be that daring moment when Woody tried a lateral. The fullback would run up the rear-end of his right guard about forty times, and the Buckeyes would win again but some sane, orderly score like 13–0.

Woody, meanwhile, lived without friends. His closest associate was a blackboard with circles and x's on it, or a film projector. He breathed football the way he breathed fire on the practice field, which was excessively. In practices, Woody was seen to bite his wrist when a Buckeye blew an assignment. He would throw his baseball cap down and stomp on it. He would hit himself in the jaw with his fist. He would growl, grumble and groan. He would slam a lineman on the shoulder pad and read him out for all the world to hear. If he thought it might rain on Saturday, he would hold practices in the rain. If he thought it might be muddy on Saturday, he would hold practices in the mud. If he felt it might snow on

Saturday, he would order a practice blizzard down from the Lord on Wednesday.

"As Admiral Doenitz said, if you're going to fight in the North Atlantic, you've got to train in the North Atlantic," Woody explained to a big tackle one afternoon, a lineman who had been shivering and sneezing — and complaining.

"Coach," the player said. "Can't we fight in Florida?"

There was this time one spring when the hard work that coaches do in the off-season was ended; spring practices were over and so was recruiting. It was the leisurely period of the year when men took vacations or played golf or caught up on inconsequential paper work. One of Woody's assistants had been wanting to have a dinner party at home, and he figured this was the perfect time. He invited his friends, and Woody, too, of course. It was to be an elaborate affair. But the man wasn't too surprised when the head coach said he was too busy to attend.

That evening, however, just as all of the friends began to arrive, the man, Bill Hess, got a phone call. It was Woody.

"Can you get over here right away?" Hayes said.

Bill explained that perhaps Woody had forgotten about the party that night. Could *he* come over there? What was so important? Was Woody sick? Had something happened to one of the players? No, none of this, Woody said. It was all right. But as soon as possible, could Bill come on down to the stadium office after dinner?

When Bill finally arrived about eleven o'clock, Woody was sitting in the film room, staring up at the screen, watching Ohio State win some long-forgotten victory.

"What is it, Coach? What's wrong?" Bill asked.

"Huh?" said Woody. "Oh, nothing. I just thought you might want to look at some films with me."

For all of the success that Woody gave Ohio State, a school that had hired and fired four different coaches in the ten years preceding him, things began to close in around him in the early 1960's, as if some evil, hidden forces were out to ruin him. It might have been that powers higher than he were tired of his rages, which still were resulting in Woody shoving his head through a wooden locker door. Or it might have been because the Ohio State faculty felt that overemphasis was creeping into Columbus. Whatever it was, Woody suffered.

First, his undefeated 1961 team was disallowed the treat of going to the Rose Bowl. Then the Big Ten voted in the no-red-shirt rule, which meant that an athlete could no longer "stay over" and remain eligible to play during his fifth year of college. Academic requirements for athletes at Ohio State increased.

And one day in 1966 after Woody had suffered a 4–5 season — a losing year; a rarity, of course — a small plane was seen circling over Ohio Stadium tugging a huge banner which said: GOOD-BYE WOODY.

Gradually it began to be whispered that perhaps football had passed Woody by. His tactics were too old. The game had opened up, but Woody still tried to win with three yards and a cloud of dust. He wasn't as tough, some said.

"Damn it," said Woody one day. "I'm not getting mellow. I'm the same guy I've always been, and I'll tell you this. The minute I think I'm getting *mellow*, then I'm retiring. Who ever heard of a mellow winner?"

And he retreated to Ralph Waldo Emerson.

"No law can be sacred to me but that of my nature," he quoted. "Blame is safer than praise," he quoted. Then he quoted himself, "Damn it," he said, "it all started with recruiting and that Rose Bowl thing. All anybody else had to say to a kid we wanted was, 'Son, if you go to Ohio State, you probably won't ever see the Rose Bowl,' and the kid would go off to another school."

Woody thought a minute about some talented new sophomores he had managed to recruit, and he said, "I think we've got the boys to win again. I think we have the character to win again. I believe we can win again. I'll tell you what. *We will win again.*"

And it was back to Emerson.

"We have to avoid being *nice,* that's all," Woody said. "That's what I tell the boys all the time. It's this *nice*ness from people complimenting you that can be killing. It can be deceiving. Yes, sir, Emerson was hitting the ball square when he said, 'As soon as honeyed words of praise are spoken for me I feel as one who lies unprotected before his enemies.' "

Woody came back, all right.

The season was 1968, a long time since Woody had unleashed a winner with a Hopalong Cassady or a Jim Parker, or a Bob White or Bob Ferguson. Nor was he back in a cloud of dust, either. Woody had these brash sophomores who were lean and mean, and he had a new offense, a modern offense that had passing and reverses and option plays and faking. He also had a defense which hungered to find the football, devour it, bury the other guys, and win some more green Buckeye leaves to paste on the side of its helmets.

Woody was thriving with his youngsters, his Rex Kerns and Jack Tatums and Jim Stillwagons. He insisted he wasn't mellow, but he let them grow the shaggy hair, the deep sideburns and the mustaches that were in vogue for young people. And he worried about their inexperience before the big ones.

"Coaches used to say the hay's in the barn after Thursday's workout," Woody said. "Well, that's a lot of bull. You have to keep thinking right up to game time. You have to consider emotion, particularly with young kids like we've got. I'll tell them before this game, 'Now you boys just clench your fists for ten seconds as hard as you can and then take a deep breath. After that is how you're supposed to feel when you're going into a football game. Relaxed, confident but determined.'"

This was the day before Woody turned his kids loose on Purdue, then the No. 1 team, a team with Leroy Keyes and Mike Phipps. Ohio State was so relaxed, confident and determined that it held Keyes to nineteen yards, knocked Phipps out of the game, and won by 13–0. The Buckeyes were back on top.

They had "run those fat tackles" all day long, and Woody, suddenly, was the Woody of old.

When the Buckeyes came down to the final Saturday of the regular season, down to the epic battle with Michigan for the Big Ten championship and Woody's chance to return to Pasadena for the first time in ten years, he looked unchanged.

He was still a heavy man with silver-streaked hair and glasses who wore those white short-sleeved shirts in freezing weather; who jabbered on and on about "paying the price" and "dedication" and what Admiral Doenitz or Lightning Joe Collins or George Patton would do in a moment of crisis.

"A good general always makes you search for his weaknesses," said Woody, plotting his strategy for Michigan.

He didn't have any, of course, because Rex Kern and Jack Tatum, his quarterback on offense and his hard-hitting spiritual leader of the defense, beat the Wolverines 50–14 and were Rose Bowl bound.

Kern, who was redheaded and freckled and kept a sly squint in his eyes like your neighborhood prankster, ran the plays off so fast Woody couldn't send them in from the sideline. Kern ran, passed, faked, blocked and hurled himself into tacklers, bouncing up, clapping his hands, chattering like a wild, frenzied savage having the time of his life. Jack Tatum, meanwhile, was everywhere, jarring loose the ball, making runners slip down at the mere sight of him.

Tatum proved that Woody was ahead of the game, not letting it pass him by. In an era of flashy offense and high-scoring, with everybody's emphasis on attacking, passing and trickery, Woody had put one of his best athletes, Tatum, on defense. Tatum could have been his top runner; his tailback. But Jack Tatum was more important to the team as a rover-back who slowed other teams down, or, in fact, stopped them cold.

Woody stood on a chair in the locker room that afternoon after Michigan had been humiliated, with Hopalong Cassady right there beside him, and said, "This team is our greatest ever. I mean that."

If Southern California, which had O. J. Simpson, was not in full accord with Woody's statement at the time it soon would be. The Trojans thought of themselves as No. 1, seeing as how they had a 9–0–1 record compared to Hayes's 9–0, and these two unbeatens were going to meet each other in the Rose Bowl. They would find out for themselves the hard way.

Woody took his team to Pasadena as if it were on a dire mission. No tours. No friends around. No Disneyland. No hanging around the movie lots. Very few interviews and pictures.

"We're out here to play a football game that's very important to us," Woody explained. "The only fun of being here will be *winning* that game."

It looked for a while like Woody might not have any fun at all on a beautifully clear, smog-free and exhilarating day when the kickoff came on New

Year's. O.J. and the Trojans ran up a 10–0 point lead, mostly on Simpson's footwork. He blew around end, faked Tatum and several other Buckeyes, and dashed eighty yards for one touchdown. He took a short, flat pass and sprinted it down into position for a field goal.

In the second and third quarters, however, with Woody prowling the sidelines, bellowing at the officials, slapping his thighs with his black cap, and with Rex Kern going to work on his passing, and runners like Jim Otis tearing into USC's middle, the Buckeyes laid on twenty points and took charge of the game. They never really stopped Simpson (he got one hundred and seventy yards), but he alone wasn't enough for Woody's brigade, and Ohio State came away with a richly deserved 27–16 victory — and Woody's fourth national championship.

"*You* didn't think our kids were going to let this slip away from them *now*, did you?" said Woody.

So he was all the way back to where he had been before — indomitable, insufferable, unmellow, unnice, insatiable — but strangely fascinating and mysteriously wonderful.

You felt, somehow, that there would always be a Woody as long as there was a Middle America and wars that Middle Americans could fight for him.

# 14

## The President's Game of the Decade

*The day Richard Nixon created chaos in the Ozarks.*

**A**LL week long in Texas the people had said that Hogs ain't nuthin' but groceries, and all week long in Arkansas the people had said that King Kong, meaning Texas's mighty No. 1 football team, ain't nuthin' but a growed-up monkey. And so everybody was in the proper spirit for the President's Game of the Decade and, more importantly where Texans and Razorbacks were concerned, *their* game of a lifetime. As one fellow modestly put it early in the week, "If the damn game don't hurry up and get here, I'm gone keel myself."

Throughout a hundred years of the sport, there had never been a situation quite like it. The fates had dictated that in this very last regular season game of 1969 — of a whole century, in fact — two brilliant

teams were coming together that were not only undefeated and untied but also were rated No. 1 and
No. 2 in the national polls. And if this wasn't enough
to drive everyone mad, then President Richard
Nixon, an old Whittier College tackle who had never
lost his fondness for the game, chose to add the final
touch that would.

Nixon announced a week ahead of time that he
would attend the contest down in that thundering
zoo of Fayetteville, Arkansas, down in that creaking
old stadium that would hold only 44,000 if everybody stood on one foot and didn't bring along their
pet pigs in their little red sweaters. And not only was
the President going to be in the stadium, he was
going to bring along a special plaque that he would
present to the winning team, either Darrell Royal's
Longhorns or Frank Broyles's Razorbacks, as the
national champion that wound up football's first one
hundred years.

It would be a hellacious football game, to be sure,
but for Fayetteville, Arkansas, it would merely be
the climax of a week-long metamorphosis — from
the nation's No. 2 chicken producer to its sports
capital. But the kickoff would come none too soon
for the town's economy was just about to suffer
badly.

"I was tryin' to sell a suit today," the manager of a

men's store said on Wednesday, "and that feller and me started talkin' about the game, and he walked out and didn't buy a thing."

The poor man stared out of his display window, which was all decorated with the red and white crepe paper of Arkansas, and said, "What's happenin' is, you wake up in the mornin' and your first thought is 'how many days to go?' "

The mania grew like a strawberry rash. Hog fever, they called it. Its symbol was Arkansas's mascot, a rather unhandsome razorback. Poster likenesses with various exhortations to Hog supremacy, appeared in most of Fayetteville's store fronts. Then a large sign went up at the First Baptist Church: ATTENTION DARRELL ROYAL — DO NOT CAST YOUR STEERS BEFORE THE SWINE.

Royal heard about it in Austin and said, "I thought God was neutral?"

"He ought to know this is the Lord's home state," replied Andrew Hall, the First Baptist pastor. "Whoever heard of a Garden of Eden in *Texas?*"

This was the same pastor who had received national attention four years earlier by posting a sign on his church before another big Texas-Arkansas game, a sign which said: FOOTBALL IS ONLY A GAME. SPIRITUAL THINGS ARE ETERNAL. NEVERTHELESS, BEAT TEXAS!

By midweek local newspapers were layers of cartoon ads showing galloping Hogs and moribund Texas Steers. "May the Steers rest in peace with our perpetual care plan. Lots $80 and up. Beat Texas. Forest Park Cemetery," said one notice.

It was extremely difficult at this point to find anyone in the town of 30,000 who did not wear a Go Hogs button of some kind, even elderly ladies and farmers in overalls.

To switch on the radio in one's hotel room or rented car was to hear practically the only song played, a lively country-Western tune by a group called Cecil Profet and the Buffaloes. Its title: "Short Squashed Texan." Its refrain:

> *I'm a short squashed Texan,*
> *I had the Number One crown.*
> *Now people look and say.*
> *That big red pig, he put you down.*

To lift the phone was to be greeted in the following manner:

"Beat Texas. Long distance."

"Beat Texas. Reservations desk."

"Beat Texas. First Baptist Church."

"Beat Texas. Holiday Inn."

Compounding the madness, of course, was the President's visit, which would mark the first time in history that a commander in chief had ever been anywhere near Fayetteville.

"I've never seen such tension in the air," said a waitress. "Imagine, almost anyone I wait on could be a secret service man. I just hope I get frisked."

Said a grinning taxi driver, "As far as I'm concerned this is the biggest thing that's happened since Johnny Cash came last year."

Every hour there was some new rumor. Billy Graham was coming to say the invocation. (He indeed was.) Johnny Cash was coming. Glen Campbell was coming. Buck Owens was coming. Roy Clark was coming because somebody *knew* he'd ordered two whole barbecued steers and six cases of whisky for the weekend.

Nixon's presence, of course, would overshadow the country music celebrities. Barely. What this meant, among other things, however, was that Arkansas had to scare up some room in its stadium — room it obviously didn't have. Bleachers were erected for 50 White House press corps members, each of whom had to be supplied with his own telephone line. Forty other seats for Nixon's entourage had to be found. And good ones.

Arkansas's fans volunteered them and accepted some terrible tradeout seats in return, getting fourteen from Darrell Royal, who said none of the Texas allotment was "worth a damn, anyway." Only five thousand seats were given to Texas, a university of thirty thousand students. And only six hundred of those were for actual students, the rest going to alumni. And of the six hundred, exactly two hundred eighty-eight had to be for the Longhorn band, which meant that only three hundred twelve real-life students would get to see the biggest game in the annals of Texas football.

"It's just as well I'm not going," said a Texas coed. "Arkansas is a hicky place. All they do is sell jelly and cider by the side of the road."

Meanwhile, in Austin one heard that things had been slightly more sophisticated but nonetheless frantic. There had been the usual banners draped across campus buildings, little gems of wisdom which said: STEERS SNOW HOGS AND SKI NO. 1, and HOGS AIN'T NUTHIN' BUT GROCERIES, and BEAT NOTRE DAME (the winner would get to play the Fighting Irish in the Cotton Bowl), and WE'LL HAVE HOG MEAT WITH WORSTER-SPEYRER SAUCE, a horrendous pun taking its meaning from two fine Texas players, Steve Worster, a fullback, and Cotton Speyrer, a split end.

More than 35,000 had turned out on a Wednesday night to see the No. 1 team and its coaches driven around the track of Memorial Stadium in convertibles while the band, over and over, drummed out "The Eyes of Texas."

Texas's insatiable fans should have known that the Arkansas game is always a blood-letting even when a mere Southwest Conference championship was riding on it, which it usually was. They should have known that the Longhorns, No. 1 or not, would be lucky to escape Fayetteville with their skin and hair and even a one-point victory. But the weeks preceding the game had clouded their thinking, and Royal felt they were getting impossible. He didn't like to see them so buoyed up by the knowledge that Texas had buried all six of the two teams' common opponents by much fatter scores with its first string rarely playing more than one half. He didn't like to hear all sorts of wonderful statistics quoted, like, for instance, Texas had become the second all-time rushing team in college history, averaging about 370 yards a game. He didn't like to hear it repeated that Texas was averaging forty points a game, or hear Texans joke that if Nixon didn't arrive early in the first quarter he might miss seeing the Longhorns' first string.

"Listen," said Royal, after his squad arrived with him on Friday. "They're gonna come after us with their eyes pulled up like BB's, and they'll be defending every foot as if Frank has told 'em there's a four hundred-foot drop just behind 'em into a pile of rocks. If you *believe* that, you're pretty hard to move around."

Instant traffic jams were already developing around the Arkansas campus and stadium on Friday afternoon. Students were just driving, going nowhere, honking and hollering, waving beer cans and Confederate flags, their roadsters painted red and white, their hands uplifted in the "V" sign.

I was driving Darrell back to his motel after the Friday workout, and he looked around at all of the Razorback revelry as we moved along, and he started working up his mad for the game; putting on his "game face," as he liked to call it. "Only angry people win football games," he had often said. And he believed that if *he* got angry every Saturday, his team would get angry.

"To hell with Arkansas," he said. "What the heck does this place have? A low per-capita income . . . pig farmers . . ." Royal owned resort property in Arkansas and had a number of close friends there, including Frank Broyles, and he liked to go there to spend a week playing golf, but he chose not to think about any of that just now. There was a game to play, a great big fantastic game that had grown into what Duffy Daugherty once said of a big game: "It's not a matter of life and death. It's more important than that."

"Look at that," Darrell said, pointing to a carload of Arkansas fans giving the "V" sign. "They don't know that means peace. A lot of things haven't gotten up here yet."

"This whole week has been fairly colorful," he was told.

"To hell with Arkansas," he said.

It was Texas, trapped in the din and wild speckled red of that stadium, which, as you might guess, almost went to blazes.

For three quarters Arkansas did everything right and Texas did everything wrong. The Razorbacks had a slender, cool quarterback named Bill Montgomery (who came from Texas) and he could pass and run with the best in the country. And what he did was pass and run the Longhorns into a state of utter shock. While a furious Arkansas defense swarmed on Royal's team to cause four fumbles and two interceptions — and create the loudest explosions in the history of Arkansas — Montgomery and his roommate end, Chuck Dicus, combined to build a fourteen-point lead, which looked like the safest place for any Razorback to be since Orval Faubus rode in a motorcade.

While Texas hadn't been able to drive past Arkansas's 30-yard line, Bill Montgomery, with his father all decked out in red and swallowing tranquilizers in the stands, hurled a twenty-one-yard pass to set up a touchdown in the first quarter, and then hurled a twenty-nine-yard touchdown pass to Dicus in the third quarter and it was 14–0.

Texas had known what it was like to trail before, however. It had trailed an equally bitter foe, Oklahoma, by fourteen points earlier in the season, and James Street, the Longhorns' miracle-making quarterback who had never lost a game, had managed to bring his team back. "Mr. Excalibur," the fans called Street, whose teammates called him Slick because of his good looks, flashy clothes and ball-handling. Slick had won eighteen straight games for Texas since he had become the quarterback in the third week of his junior season, and he had a way of revving up the team with his jabbering confidence.

His teammates said that in moments of crisis Street would look everyone in the eye in the huddles and say things like "Guts up time . . . Gotta go . . . Gotta get 'em . . . no fumblin' . . . everbody get his man . . . Suck it up, suck it up . . . Gotta go . . . We're the best . . ." And he would keep it up until somebody like big Bob McKay, the All-

America tackle, would say, "Aw, James, shut up and call the play."

Somehow, some way, in the midst of all of that chaos in the Ozarks, with the season-long battle for No. 1 now shrunk down to the last fifteen minutes of the very last game, James Street would find a way for Texas, and pull out a glorious 15–14 victory on a day that would be remembered forever.

Upstairs in the world's most crowded little press box where the President had moved at half time to chat on national television with ABC's announcers, Chris Schenkel and Bud Wilkinson, a most miserable man stood holding hands, for luck, with a pretty young girl.

He was Jones Ramsey, the good-natured Texas publicity man, and she was Barbara Specht, a lovely blonde coed from Texas Tech who had reigned all season as the Centennial Queen of College Football.

Barbara looked as worried and grim as Ramsey. "I hate to be partial,' she said. "But after all, I *am* a Texan. This game just means so much to everybody, I can't stand it."

Ramsey managed a smile and said, "I'll tell you. I'm a coward and I believe in all kinds of jinxes, but maybe James Street doesn't. We still got time."

Along about now, down there at the Arkansas 42-

yard line, James Street was drifting back to try a pass. Suddenly, he began to run. He ran through the line, cut to the left, then back to his right, and he was rolling through the Razorbacks' secondary, his white uniform with the burnt orange trim a blur against the bright green Astroturf. Now he was carving an angle across the field, and then turning toward the Arkansas goal — either that, or the Presidential helicopter moored on a practice field just outside the end zone. In any case, Street was gone, and nobody was about to catch him. It was the first daylight Texas had seen all afternoon, and Street made the most of it.

Quickly, then, Street lined up his team for an unconventional two-point try after the touchdown. He took the snap, darted to his left, then cut inside and wiggled through a cluster of red jerseys, and flopped over the goal. James Street had personally got Texas eight points. It was 14–8, and as suddenly as anything else, this was the old Texas-Arkansas type of game that everyone knew and loved.

"I was gonna throw a hook," James explained later. "But their linebacker had my eyes fogged. I couldn't see any receivers, so I decided to run. Sure glad."

Although Street's two dazzling plays had certainly put Texas back in the ball game — and Texas's hopes began to glimmer — Arkansas wasn't finished. Bill

Montgomery stormed the Razorbacks right back down the field, seventy-three gnawing yards, to Texas's 7-yard line. The crowd was no more delirious than any normal audience for Johnny Cash. It gave off long choruses of Whoooooo, Pig, soooooey, the Arkansas yell.

If Arkansas did the right thing now, it was all over. You knew that. It was third down, only ten minutes to play. Surely the Razorbacks would run into the line, shoving into position for a field goal that would make the score 17–8, a margin too great, no doubt, for the Longhorns to overcome. But Arkansas didn't do that. Weirdly, the call to Montgomery from Arkansas's offensive coach Don Breaux, calling all the plays from a booth upstairs, was a flat pass. And when Texas got a hard rush on Montgomery, he threw late for Chuck Dicus, and Texas's Danny Lester spurted in front of the end to intercept in the end zone. Texas was still alive.

The Longhorns moved the ball but couldn't score on that drive because of a *fifth* fumble, but when they got the ball again seventy-four yards away from the Arkansas goal and only six minutes left, James Street and Darrell Royal — the whole world, in fact — knew that this would have to be it.

In the press box the partisan announcer from Arkansas said over his P.A. to the writers, "Fellers, if

I keep gettin' these yardages and names wrong on the play-by-play, it's just because I'm more nervous than I was on my weddin' day. This shoot-out, or whatever you want to call it, has made me a wreck."

On the first three plays of the drive Steve Worster, who somehow tore out ninety-four yards rushing during the day, made six steps, and Ted Koy made one. A fourth down had come up, with three yards needed for new life, and the ball was on Texas's own 43-yard line. Less than five minutes were left. If Texas punted, it might never see the ball again. It had to gamble.

The Longhorns called time-out and Street went to the sideline to confer with Darrell Royal.

"Can you get it on the keep?" asked Royal.

"Yeah," said Street.

"Is Steve tired?" the coach wondered.

"Nobody's tired," said James.

Royal looked up at the scoreboard clock and the down and distance.

James said, "*They're* gettin' tired, Coach. I think we can option 'em."

"Hit Peschel deep," said Royal.

"Huh?" said Street.

"Tight end deep," Royal said.

Street started onto the field, stopped, and came back.

"Are you sure you want to throw, Coach?" he said.

Royal nodded and waved him onto the field, and turned and walked away.

When Street got to the huddle and started jabbering about how this might be Texas's last play of the season, and then called the pass play, saying he thought they could surprise Arkansas with a long bomb to the tight end, Bob McKay shrieked.

"Geeaad, damn, James. You cain't *throw* it that far," he said.

"Gimme some time and I'll get it there," said Street. "Randy," he added, looking his end in the eye. "This is it."

Street tossed the forty-four-yard spiral perfectly to Randy Peschel, who took the ball in full stride over his shoulder and collapsed out of bounds on Arkansas's 13-yard line. And in two piercing ground plays Texas's Jim Bertelsen barged into the end zone, and then Happy Feller place-kicked the extra point that made it 15–14.

"In a case like that," said Darrell Royal of the desperate pass that Street gambled with, "there's no logic. You don't know what to call. You just suck it up and pick a number. And it doesn't hurt to have James Street playing for you."

Thus, a team had labored all day under more pressure than any No. 1 team ever had, and then with time running out, on alien ground, with few friends about, with a whole century closing in, that team had somehow survived.

And it was properly ready to go meet a President.

# 15

## The Immortals

*In a hundred years we were not exactly devoid of heroes.*

To those of us who have studied and followed college football over the years as closely as we have the hemlines of our secretaries and airline stewardesses and who have devoted a great many hours to genuflecting before its shrines — Darrell Royal's pride building, for example, or John McKay's wit — the first hundred years seems to have sped by as quickly as O. J. Simpson did on hut-hut 23-Blast, or whatever that thing was he did so often. One day there were just those pioneers from Princeton and Rutgers and then a whole mosaic of the game unfolded like a card section spelling out Granny Rice. Here came Pudge Heffelgrange, Amos Alonzo Baugh, Crazy Legs Heisman, Slingin' Sammy Nevers, the Seven Blocks of Seats, Fireball Frankie Harmon, Mr.

Sideways and Mr. Backwards, Win One for the Gifford, Indian Doak Thorpe, all of those marvelous coaching names: Pop, Jock, Dutch, Red, Tiny, Moose, Biff and Biggie, all inventing Old 83, the Flea Flopper, and always like a breath of fire and a streak of flame outlined against a dull gray October schedule, as Rice wrote, here came General George (Blood and Guts) Hayes and his Buckeyes, or St. Darrell and his Longhorns, to win again.

It seems impossible that we would have had none of this had it not been for those inventive men from Princeton and Rutgers, twenty-five on a side, who removed their waistcoats back on Nov. 6, 1869 and fell into a heap; that without their efforts Texas would have met Arkansas on the Astroturf of Fayetteville, Arkansas, in a televised debate to see who was No. 1 in English Lit 341; that Walter Camp might have been the Father of American Crew; that the annual Army-Navy spectacle might now alternate between lacrosse fields at West Point and Annapolis; and that the Crimson Tide would roll, tide, roll, largely during Southeastern Conference triangular track meets.

Unthinkable. If no one else had, Notre Dame would surely have invented football later on, and each season would then be a giddy anniversary of

Knute Rockne's first fingertip catch on a wobbler from Gus Dorais.

Of course, it took more minds than just those of Princeton and Rutgers to develop college football into the slightly paranoid religion it became: a game watched by paying millions who worship a galloping goose one season and fire his jolly old coach the next. Harvard and Yale had much to do with its early sophistication, as I have hinted earlier. Without them we might never have had the scoring we know, the snapback, eleven men to a side or picnics by station wagon. Notre Dame gave us the true intersectional schedule and introduced the enormous dividends of winning. A group of Californians gave us the bowl game. A man from St. Louis devised the forward pass, and the Southwest made it a major weapon. The Deep South thought up frantic defense, and the Midwest originated the brute. It was also the Midwest that dragged the game out of the East, forcing Walter Camp to acknowledge All-Americas west of the Statue of Liberty. If Bear Bryant actually originated effort, Bud Wilkinson invented speed and magic. Recruiting was older than Frank Leahy; it was as old as Pudge Heffelfinger and Germany Schulz. And in one hundred years nobody figured out a way to beat the team that had the studs, if the studs felt like exerting themselves on Saturday afternoons.

There got to be a saying that pro football had become the national game, one insinuation being that baseball no longer was and another being that college football was no more than a farm system in the 60's. But, before this could be a fact, the pros had to answer some questions. Such as: What pro player caused more excitement and received more publicity than a collegian named O.J.? Before him, what pro player got more national attention than Roger Staubach at Navy? Ernie Davis at Syracuse? Billy Cannon at LSU? Howard Cassady at Ohio State? If there were so many coaching geniuses in the pros, why was Vince Lombardi the only one who ever won? How many pro clubs would like to draw the repetitious crowds of Ohio State, Notre Dame, USC, Texas, LSU, Michigan State, Georgia Tech, Alabama, Arkansas and many others? No one could pick a regular-season pro game that could out-Nielsen a poll bowl, even if it wasn't Notre Dame vs. USC, and why did Ohio State continue to get its 81,000 at home whether its quarterback threw a pass in the air or in the dirt?

What was actually true was that football, college and pro, had become the national game, each variety enhancing the other's prestige. But it was also true that the colleges could do without the pros, as they did for years. Pro football was beautiful, to be sure — the avid fan liked all phases of his game — but the pros still only sold the bomb and the mystique of the double Z-out, while the college game, armed with its vast head start in tradition, had both of these plus more triple options and monster rovers than the fan (or the writer) would ever comprehend, not to forget so many other things: the raccoon coat, the pregame party, the postgame party, the half time, girls, cheerleaders, fight songs, homecoming, All-Americas, the effigy, the bowls, who's No. 1, pursuit, the button-down shirt and all of those years of lore, all of those breaths of fire and streaks of flame galloping through the swollen heart of Clyde (Old) Grad, season ticket holder No. 46,567, his lovely wife Mavis, an ex-twirler, and his son, Bubba, who'll start at fullback for Super-Suburb High.

College football will always endure and prosper with legend. The stars never die, and hundreds of games live on. Classics, they are called. Those who saw them still hear the thunder of Texas-Arkansas in 1969, of USC-UCLA in 1967, of Notre Dame-Michigan State in 1966, of Army-Notre Dame in 1946, of Minnesota-Michigan in 1940, of Pitt-Fordham in

1937, of TCU-SMU in 1935 and of as many Army-Navys and Alabama-Tennessees as you care to count. Old 77 is still delivering ice for the Illini. Old 98 is still cruising down the sidelines for the Wolverines. Billy Cannon is still returning that punt against Ole Miss on a Halloween Night in Baton Rouge. They're still totaling up the magazine covers that Doak Walker made at SMU. It took a lot of Morley Drurys to make O.J. the noblest Trojan. Harry Stuhldreher begat Frank Carideo who begat Angelo Bertelli who begat Johnny Lujack who begat Ralph Guglielmi who begat Paul Hornung who begat Terry Hanratty at Notre Dame. At Texas, future Longhorns will try to "dance every dance" like Tommy Nobis or James Street did. And Joe Namath was wearing white shoes and blowing it in for six at Alabama long before he ever found his way to Broadway.

We can estimate that more than two and a half million men played college football in the first one hundred years and that about fifteen hundred were immortal, which is to say All-America. At least as many immortals were overlooked for All-America, no doubt, because they didn't wear their socks high or have a colorful nickname or work for a publicity-minded coach or have a Granny Rice writing poems about them. How could a halfback be a breath of fire and a streak of flame playing for, say, Southwestern

Louisiana, for example? And yet Chris Cagle became something akin to that when he went on to Army for four more years of college ball back in the 1920's when you could do that sort of thing, the rules being rather lax.

With so many greats, near-greats, semi-greats and would-have-beens handed down to us through the years, it would not seem likely that any select group of them could have been better than all the rest at their positions as collegians. And yet some were. Although coaches enjoy saying you can't compare athletes because size, speed, technique and emphasis change, in a way you can. Desire and instinct do not change, nor does that strange inspired ability an athlete can possess that will lift his team above itself.

Thus, there *have* been those players who combined these traits to win consistently against major competition, which is of no small importance in measuring greatness, who sparkled all the more when they were thrust into stardom, who literally seemed to relish the dramatic situation and most often conquered it. Therefore, by all that I know of college football's history and what I believe to be true of legend, and from all that I have personally seen and heard, these were the truest immortals of the decades:

## THE FIRST 50 YEARS

E — *Frank Hinkey*, Yale
E — *Tack Hardwick*, Harvard
T — *Wilbur Henry*, Washington & Jefferson
T — *Belf West*, Colgate
G — *Pudge Heffelfinger*, Yale
G — *T. Truxton Hare*, Pennsylvania
C — *Bob Peck*, Pittsburgh
B — *Walter Eckersall*, Chicago
B — *Jim Thorpe*, Carlisle
B — *Willie Heston*, Michigan
B — *Ted Coy*, Yale

## THE TWENTIES

E — *Bennie Oosterbaan*, Michigan
E — *Brick Muller*, California
T — *Bronko Nagurski*, Minnesota
T — *Ed Weir*, Nebraska
G — *Dutch Diehl*, Dartmouth
G — *Jack Cannon*, Notre Dame
C — *Peter Pund*, Georgia Tech
B — *George Gipp*, Notre Dame
B — *Red Grange*, Illinois
B — *Chris Cagle*, Army
B — *Ernie Nevers*, Stanford

## THE THIRTIES

E — *Don Hutson*, Alabama
E — *Gaynell Tinsley*, LSU
T — *Ed Widseth*, Minnesota

T — *Bruiser Kinard*, Mississippi
G — *Bob Suffridge*, Tennessee
G — *Joe Routt*, Texas A&M
C — *Ki Aldrich*, TCU
B — *Sam Baugh*, TCU
B — *Tom Harmon*, Michigan
B — *Clint Frank*, Yale
B — *Marshall Goldberg*, Pittsburgh

## THE FORTIES

E — *Leon Hart*, Notre Dame
E — *Barney Poole*, Mississippi
T — *George Connor*, Notre Dame
T — *Dick Wildung*, Minnesota
G — *Alex Agase*, Illinois
G — *Bill Fischer*, Notre Dame
C — *Chuck Bednarik*, Pennsylvania
B — *Johnny Lujack*, Notre Dame
B — *Doak Walker*, SMU
B — *Glenn Davis*, Army
B — *Doc Blanchard*, Army

## THE FIFTIES

E — *Ron Beagle*, Navy
E — *Ron Kramer*, Michigan
T — *Alex Karras*, Iowa
T — *Lou Michaels*, Kentucky
G — *Les Richter*, California
G — *Jim Parker*, Ohio State
C — *Jerry Tubbs*, Oklahoma

B — *Dick Kazmaier*, Princeton
B — *Jim Swink*, TCU
B — *Howard Cassady*, Ohio State
B — *Billy Cannon*, LSU

### THE SIXTIES

E — *George Webster*, Michigan State
E — *Jerry Levias*, SMU
T — *Ron Yary*, USC
T — *Bobby Bell*, Minnesota
G — *Tommy Nobis*, Texas
G — *Dick Butkus*, Illinois
C — *Lee Roy Jordan*, Alabama
B — *James Street*, Texas
B — *Gale Sayers*, Kansas
B — *Ernie Davis*, Syracuse
B — *O. J. Simpson*, USC

It isn't a bad list and if you want to consider them the sixty-six greatest men who ever played the college game, so be it. But I will go even further, undaunted, and risk the wrath of assorted immortals from South Bend to Tuscaloosa, and all of our far-flung old grads. I believe there were *eleven* players who were truer immortals than the rest. Call it an All-Century Team if you like. That's what I call it.

Basically it is a modern team, and that does not seem improper. Mental strain became a great part of football after mid-century. The pressure to excel in packed stadiums and against the ponderous weight of headlines had become enormous. Excessively. We shall never know what Willie Heston might have done, going for No. 1 before 90,000 in the Los Angeles Coliseum, for example, but we *do* know what O. J. Simpson did.

It is a team whose members share a number of distinctions. Eight players, for instance, have been chosen by various reputable selectors on Alltime teams. They would be Sam Baugh, Red Grange, Don Hutson, Bronko Nagurski, Bennie Oosterbaan, George Connor, Bob Suffridge and Bob Peck. Each of the eleven was an All-America, naturally, most of them twice and five of them — Doak Walker, Grange, Oosterbaan, Suffridge and Peck — three times. Walker is football's last three-year consensus All-America. Eight of the men led their teams to at least one undefeated season, and seven of them played on mythical national champions.

But let us look at them individually.

Sam Baugh of Texas Christian was everything a quarterback should be and something few of them have been since his day. Joe Namath is the only passer who has come along that anyone would dare suggest could throw the ball as well as Sam. But Baugh was also perhaps the finest punter who ever arched his foot. For example, in the Sugar Bowl game of 1936 against LSU, on a rainy day, Baugh punted fourteen times, frequently within LSU's 5-yard line, for a forty-eight-yard average.

Wiry and tobacco-chewing, Sam had the con artist in him, as a leader on the field who also played a vicious safety on defense. Once, when TCU was playing Tulsa, his fullback obviously scored, but an official disallowed it. "You're exactly right, Mr. Referee," said Sam quickly. "I saw it and he didn't get over." Whereupon, Sam called his own number on the next play, and this time the referee's hands went up for a touchdown almost before Baugh could take the snap.

Slingin' Sam threw long and short, soft and hard, dancing, running, being hit or with his feet planted. In an era when ten passes in a game was considered extravagant, Baugh hurled thirty and forty, hit most of his receivers in the bridge of the nose and spiraled an unbelievable (then) thirty-eight touchdowns in three seasons.

Grantland Rice was so taken with Sam and the dazzling style of football that TCU played that he went on picking Dutch Meyer's teams in his pre-season Top Ten for years after Baugh left.

Another Baugh never turned up in the Southwest, but a Doak Walker did. Walker did more things well in football, including win — win with a mediocre team — than just about anyone who ever played. He ran, passed, punted, caught, place-kicked, blocked and defended. And, in an era of free subs, he would play most of a tough game, both ways.

Handsome and shy off the field, graceful, calm and dramatic under pressure, he was everything the magazine covers yearned for, and the Cotton Bowl got double-decked because of his deeds for SMU. His most familiar play would be to get trapped trying to pass and then weave off a long run. Doak had that wonderful talent for making a five-yard run seem like thirty, and his sixty-yarders seemed to take an hour, for he faked, dodged and bewildered everyone in the stadium along the way.

In everything he tried, the form was always perfect, and among other things his sleekness was all the more noticeable by the fact that he was the first player in my memory to wear low-quarter shoes. If you wanted a seventy-yard quick kick, Doak kicked it. If you wanted a thirty-yard field goal, he kicked that, too. He would raise up and complete a pass on one play, then leap up and catch one from somebody else. And best of all, he would find a way to win, frequently in the closing minutes. They called him "the miracle man," and he was precisely that in an age of perhaps the strongest football (the late 1940's) we have seen.

The miracle man of the 1920's was Red Grange, of course. Primarily an open-field runner — and by all evidence the best ever — this led to a joke that has become part of football lore. Before Grange's famed Michigan game of 1924 when he scored five touchdowns and gained 402 yards (including returns), the Wolverines' daily newspaper had said, "All Grange can do is run." And the *Daily Illini* had rebutted, "All Galli-Curci can do is sing."

Grange's style was not to waste motion and he had a freedom of movement. He would start wide, cut back, then cut back again, carving a big S on the field. He once said his mind tried to envision where his teammates were and what they were doing as he ran and he would somehow use them. "I could see the run happening as I ran," he explained.

Grange had real speed for his day, a fast start, excellent balance and the uncanny ability — peripheral vision, they called it in Doak Walker's day — to see tacklers coming from the sides.

Knute Rockne complained that much of Grange's success was due to "skillful exploiting in the papers," but he *did* make all of those runs for three years, and he later turned them into big money. He endorsed everything he could find, including cigarettes he did not smoke, which could have invoked one of the marvelous ad slogans of all time: "If Red Grange smoked, he'd smoke Philip Morris!"

As much as Grange ran, he did not come near running as often as O.J. did at USC. Nor has anyone else in just two years. Or against such consistently rugged opposition, much of it stacked against him. As it has been said before, no runner in college ever combined speed, power, elusiveness and endurance like Simpson. All he did was gain about 3,500 yards in twenty-two games (counting Rose Bowls), scoring thirty-six touchdowns.

Over and over, O.J. made holes where there weren't any and created daylight out of tangled jerseys. Not only was he 6′ 2″ and more than 200 pounds, he had 9.4 speed and moves. And never had a fast man carried so often, up to forty times a game. In the ninety-ninth season of college football he was, appropriately enough, all of the greatness that had come before him in one dynamic package.

It has never been easy for a lineman to achieve glory, as most fans are aware, for in football most of the romance thrives on dazzling runs and accurate passes. Baugh, Walker, Grange and Simpson proved it, as have so many others. But a few have risen from the gore of the scrimmage line and remained giants ever since. The player on my All-Century team who goes back the farthest is the center, Bob Peck of Pittsburgh, who was one of the best at focusing attention on himself.

One reason was that he taped his wrists, ankles and headgear so there would be no mistaking him in a heap. Small but outrageously aggressive, Peck yelling could often be heard high up in the stands, and, when he made tackle after tackle and kept up the chatter and fierce mannerisms, a Pitt whoop got started: "When Peck fights, the team fights."

With Peck at center, Pitt lost only one game from 1914 through 1916; and the last team was not only the national champion, Pop Warner said it was the greatest he ever coached.

The guards who flanked Bob Peck were the same type of fanatics. One needs to say little else of Tennessee's Bob Suffridge except that General Bob Neyland considered him the greatest lineman he ever had. Suffridge was a moody, antagonistic player who could hardly eat or speak on the day of a game. Best of the pulling single wing guards, he was a defensive terror as well. The Vols did not lose a regular-season game in the three years that Suffridge made All-America, 1938 through 1940. As for the other guard, it is doubtful if ever there breathed a more dedicated player than Texas's Tommy Nobis, who had size and ability to go with it. He had a fire that was usually found in players trying to compensate for lack of size — like Peck or Suffridge.

"He simply never made a bad play," said his coach, Darrell Royal. "I've never seen any player handle his position so well — or ever heard of one."

Nobis was primarily a linebacker of the type who averaged twenty or so tackles a game, who was everywhere, quick, strong, nimble and eager, but who also, in a platoon era, went over to offense when the goal line got into view. Much to his credit is the fact that Nobis was at his best against the big names he faced — Namath, Roger Staubach and Donny Anderson among others — and Nobis won.

Notre Dame was always up to its Dome in immortals at all positions and, if you said, O.K., the Irish could have all eleven of the Alltime team, South Benders wouldn't be able to agree on most of the names. One guy would be a cinch, however. Notre Dame never had a better tackle than George Connor, and if big George is the best Notre Dame ever had, then he must be better than nearly all the others.

A blocker who opened gaps for the Johnny Lujacks and Terry Brennans, he was a crushing defender who moved from one side to the other to put the brakes on runners like Buddy Young. Big and mobile, he was a leader who had a sense of humor.

Once, before a great big Army game, he told the team, "The sons of slum and gravy are coming to the campus of beans and sausage."

"He had the agility to sort out the ballcarrier and the toughness to break up the power play," said Frank Leahy. "He was indestructible."

So apparently was my other tackle, Bronko Nagurski, who was more than just a tackle. For Minnesota, Nagurski was also a fullback and he was even an end for a time. He would have beaten out any man at any position, old Gopher fans will argue, but the experts pretty much agree that Nagurski, powerful, numb to pain, durable and inspired, played his best football at tackle, almost single-handedly raising so-so Minnesota teams into winners.

Nagurski was considered a physical brute at 6' 2" and 217, and his bravery was often displayed when he would hunker into the line to stop every play, then shift to fullback to lug the ball repeatedly. One way or another, he made the big play.

Bronko Nagurski benefited from a catchy name, to be sure, as did Grange, the Galloping Ghost. Between them in the Big Ten, there was a player who had a name to overcome — Bennie Oosterbaan. But while Oosterbaan might have been a headache for headline writers, he was the most splendid thing Michigan had ever seen.

Oosterbaan was the first of the brilliant pass catchers, an acrobatic player who dived and scooped up the ball or who one-handed it in midair. Wherever Benny Friedman threw it. It is said that he was the most complete end who ever played, that in three years of All-America performances no runner ever gained around his end. And this included Grange.

Oosterbaan was a natural type of player, fluid of motion, almost beautiful in his faking, the patterns he invented and the ease with which he gathered in the ball. Only Don Hutson, who came along in the next decade, has ever been compared with him as a receiver.

What Hutson could do better than Oosterbaan was run with the ball after he caught it. Tall and willowy with immense speed and at least four different gaits, Hutson at Alabama brought all of the dimensions of a pass receiver that we now know of to the game. "I just ran like the devil, and Dixie Howell got the ball there," Hutson said later, but he did more. The Alabama Antelope invented catching "in traffic," he made the end-around a devastating weapon and shifting gears a must. He made multiple faking vital.

While Hutson would catch only six or eight passes in a game, that was a bundle then, and they would be Alabama's key yardage, if not its touchdowns.

When he grabbed six passes for 165 yards and two touchdowns in Alabama's victory over Stanford in the 1935 Rose Bowl, he was lavishly labeled "the world's greatest pass-catching, speed-merchant end," and no one has tried to put anyone ahead of him since.

And so huddles a team to commemorate a century, a team that can speak well for the lore of a colorful game. There is a Bronko and an Antelope, a Slingin' Sam, some Orange Juice, and a Galloping Ghost. There is passing, running, kicking, receiving and wanton defense. There is speed and enough size. There are winners. But now who do they play? Well, in only one hundred more years I will let you know.

# Epilogue

SEVERAL years ago when I worked for a newspaper in Fort Worth, Texas, my hometown, I used to enjoy spending as much time as possible around a man named Abe Martin because he made me choke, stumble and very often fall down from laughter, and he never stopped giving me something to write about.

These were fairly modern times in football but Abe was a coach who lived and talked in a way that made you think he was always somewhere back in Jack County, squatting on the steps of a feed store.

Abe chewed tobacco now and then, of course, his tie was usually loose, a crumpled hat was pushed toward the back of his head and he spoke in a slow, good-natured drawl. His sentences frequently came out like this: "Aw, old Tommy Joe, he's a goooood foo-ball player, yew bet."

Foo-ball, Abe said, was not round. Foo-ball was oblong, goofy shaped.

"Now this dang foo-ball is the only game I know of that ain't played with a round ball," he said. "Foo-ball is gonna bounce on you. Folks are gonna win and folks are gonna lose, and a man's got to be a man about it."

When the sport began to get a little more sophisticated than Abe wished, he tried to pretend that it hadn't really done so.

"They talkin' about *pursuit* in foo-ball," he said one day. "Well, that ain't nuthin' but chase 'em and catch 'em."

Once Abe had a truly brilliant halfback named Jim Swink who led the major colleges in rushing and scoring and took TCU to a championship, and the coach was repeatedly asked to describe Swink's running style. "Well, he's just a little old rubber-legged outfit nobody can catch," said Abe.

Bob Lilly, whom Abe also coached, was at first "just a big old green pea," said the coach, "but he'll stand in there for you like a picket fence."

He liked little men, guys with something to prove. "Pine knots," Abe called them. "You gimme a gunnysack full of little old pine knots who'll hit-chee and we'll have us a spellin' bee come Saturday," is the way Abe would put it.

A foo-ball game to Abe was not always a spellin'
bee. Sometimes it was a choir practice, a formal
dance, an ear roastin' or a story tellin'.

I specifically remember this clear, chilled autumn
day when Abe and I were strolling around on the
stadium floor at TCU about half an hour before a big
game against the University of Texas. The stands
were filled, the bands were playing, and the two
teams were warming up as the sun beamed down on
the rich purple jerseys of TCU and the orange shirts
of Texas.

We walked slowly along the sideline, just looking
around, breathing in the clean air, enjoying the tension and the excitement that builds toward an opening kickoff. Abe had his hands stuck in the pockets of
his lucky brown suit.

"Well, all you can say now, Coach, is that this is
liable to be a formal dance," I said.

"Aw, yew bet," said Abe. "Today we're gonna have
us a *sheep shearin'* out here on this *foo-ball* field."

Abe walked on a few steps and then paused and
sort of stretched and looked all around the stadium.

"Danny," he said. "You know what that is up there
in those stands and down here on this foo-ball field?
What we got around us here is the greatest thing in
the whole world. What we got here is Saturday's
America."

I knew then, all of those years ago, that a marvelous old country gentleman had given me the title of a book.

# Appendix

Here, after more research than the author cares to be
reminded of, are *all* of our No. 1 teams from college football's first 100 years:

KEY

| Positions | | | Rating Systems |
|---|---|---|---|
| qb | quarterback | AP | Associated Press (1936–1969) |
| hb | halfback | Davis | Park H. Davis Ratings (1889–1935) |
| fb | fullback | DS | Dickinson System (1924–1940) |
| lb | linebacker | Dunkel | Dunkel System (1929–1969) |
| e | end | FWA | Football Writers Association of America (1954–1969) |
| t | tackle | Helms | Helms Athletic Foundation (1889–1969) |
| g | guard | HF | National Football Hall of Fame (1959–1969) |
| c | center | IFA | Illustrated Football Annual (1924–1941) |
| | | LS | Litkenhous System (1934–1969) |
| | | TFT | The Football Thesaurus (1927–1958) |
| | | UPI | United Press International (1950–1969) |
| | | WS | Williamson System (1932–1963) |

| Year | Team & Record | Coach | Top Player | Selector |
|---|---|---|---|---|
| 1969 | TEXAS, 11–0 | Darrell Royal | James Street, qb | Unanimous |
| 1968 | OHIO STATE, 10–0 | Woody Hayes | Rex Kern, qb | Unanimous |
| 1967 | USC, 10–1 | John McKay | O. J. Simpson, hb | Unanimous |
| 1966 | NOTRE DAME, 9–0–1 | Ara Parseghian | Terry Hanratty, qb | Unanimous |

| Year | Team & Record | Coach | Top Player | Selector |
|------|---------------|-------|------------|----------|
|      | MICHIGAN STATE, 9–0–1 | Duffy Daugherty | George Webster, lb | Helms, HF (tie) |
| 1965 | MICHIGAN STATE, 10–1 | Duffy Daugherty | Clinton Jones, hb | All but AP |
|      | ALABAMA, 9–1–1 | Bear Bryant | Steve Sloan, qb | AP, FWA (tie) |
| 1964 | ALABAMA, 10–1 | Bear Bryant | Joe Namath, qb | AP, UPI, LS |
|      | ARKANSAS, 11–0 | Frank Broyles | Bobby Crockett, e | FWA, Helms |
|      | NOTRE DAME, 9–1 | Ara Parseghian | John Huarte, qb | HF |
|      | MICHIGAN, 9–1 | Bump Elliott | Bob Timberlake, qb | Dunkel |
| 1963 | TEXAS, 11–0 | Darrell Royal | Tommy Nobis, lb | Unanimous |
| 1962 | USC, 11–0 | John McKay | Pete Beathard, qb | All but LS |
|      | MISSISSIPPI, 10–0 | Johnny Vaught | Glynn Griffing, qb | LS |
| 1961 | ALABAMA, 11–0 | Bear Bryant | Lee Roy Jordan, c | All but FWA |
|      | OHIO STATE, 9–0–1 | Woody Hayes | Bob Ferguson, fb | FWA |
| 1960 | MINNESOTA, 8–2 | Murray Warmath | Sandy Stephens, qb | AP, UPI, HF |
|      | MISSISSIPPI, 10–0–1 | Johnny Vaught | Jake Gibbs, qb | FWA, WS, Dunkel |
|      | WASHINGTON, 10–1 | Jim Owens | Bob Schloredt, qb | Helms |
|      | IOWA, 8–1 | Forest Evashevski | Larry Ferguson, hb | LS |
| 1959 | SYRACUSE, 11–1 | Ben Schwartzwalder | Ernie Davis, hb | All but Dunkel |
|      | MISSISSIPPI, 10–1 | Johnny Vaught | Charlie Flowers, fb | Dunkel |
| 1958 | LSU, 11–0 | Paul Dietzel | Billy Cannon, hb | All but FWA |
|      | IOWA, 8–1–1 | Forest Evashevski | Randy Duncan, qb | FWA |
| 1957 | AUBURN, 10–0 | Shug Jordan | Red Phillips, e | AP, WS, TFT, Helms |
|      | OHIO STATE, 9–1 | Woody Hayes | Bob White, fb | UPI, FWA, LS |
|      | MICHIGAN STATE, 8–1 | Duffy Daugherty | Walt Kowalczyk, hb | Dunkel |
| 1956 | OKLAHOMA, 10–0 | Bud Wilkinson | Tommy McDonald, hb | All but TFT |
|      | GEORGIA TECH, 10–1 | Bobby Dodd | Paul Rotenberry, hb | TFT |

| Year | Team & Record | Coach | Top Player | Selector |
|---|---|---|---|---|
| 1955 | OKLAHOMA, 11–0 | Bud Wilkinson | Jerry Tubbs, c | Unanimous |
| 1954 | UCLA, 9–0 | Red Sanders | Bob Davenport, fb | UP, FWA, Dunkel, LS, Helms |
| | OHIO STATE, 10–0 | Woody Hayes | Howard Cassady, hb | AP, WS, TFT |
| 1953 | NOTRE DAME, 9–0–1 | Frank Leahy | Johnny Lattner, hb | All but AP, UPI |
| | MARYLAND, 10–1 | Jim Tatum | Bernie Faloney, qb | AP, UPI |
| 1952 | MICHIGAN STATE, 9–0 | Biggie Munn | Leroy Bolden, hb | All but TFT |
| | GEORGIA TECH, 12–0 | Bobby Dodd | Leon Hardeman, fb | TFT |
| 1951 | TENNESSEE, 10–0 | Bob Neyland | Hank Lauricella, qb | AP, UPI, LS, WS |
| | MARYLAND, 10–0 | Jim Tatum | Jack Scarbath, qb | Dunkel |
| | MICHIGAN STATE, 9–0 | Biggie Munn | Don Coleman, t | Helms |
| | GEORGIA TECH, 11–0–1 | Bobby Dodd | Lamar Wheat, t | TFT |
| 1950 | OKLAHOMA, 10–1 | Bud Wilkinson | Leon Heath, fb | All but Dunkel, TFT |
| | TENNESSEE, 11–1 | Bob Neyland | Bud Sherrod, e | Dunkel, TFT |
| 1949 | NOTRE DAME, 10–0 | Frank Leahy | Leon Hart, e | Unanimous |
| 1948 | MICHIGAN, 9–0 | Bennie Oosterbaan | Chuck Ortmann, hb | Unanimous |
| 1947 | NOTRE DAME, 9–0 | Frank Leahy | Johnny Lujack, qb | AP, WS, Helms |
| | MICHIGAN, 10–0 | Fritz Crisler | Bob Chappuis, hb | Dunkel, LS, TFT |
| 1946 | NOTRE DAME, 8–0–1 | Frank Leahy | George Connor, t | AP, Dunkel, LS |
| | ARMY, 9–0–1 | Red Blaik | Arnold Tucker, qb | Helms, TFT |
| | GEORGIA, 11–0 | Wally Butts | Charley Trippi, hb | WS |
| 1945 | ARMY, 9–0 | Red Blaik | Doc Blanchard, fb | Unanimous |
| 1944 | ARMY, 9–0 | Red Blaik | Glenn Davis, hb | Unanimous |
| 1943 | NOTRE DAME, 9–1 | Frank Leahy | Angelo Bertelli, qb | Unanimous |

| Year | Team & Record | Coach | Top Player | Selector |
|---|---|---|---|---|
| 1942 | GEORGIA, 11–1 | Wally Butts | Frank Sinkwich, hb | WS, LS, TFT |
| | OHIO STATE, 9–1 | Paul Brown | Gene Fekete, fb | AP, Dunkel |
| | WISCONSIN, 8–1–1 | Harry Stuhldreher | Dave Schreiner, e | Helms |
| 1941 | MINNESOTA, 8–0 | Bernie Bierman | Bruce Smith, hb | All but WS & TFT |
| | TEXAS, 8–1–1 | Dana X. Bible | Jack Crain, hb | WS |
| | ALABAMA, 9–2 | Frank Thomas | Holt Rast, e | TFT |
| 1940 | MINNESOTA, 8–0 | Bernie Bierman | George Franck, fb | AP, DS, LS, IFA, TFT |
| | TENNESSEE, 10–1 | Bob Neyland | Bob Suffridge, g | Dunkel, WS |
| | STANFORD, 10–0 | Clark Shaughnessy | Frankie Albert, qb | Helms |
| 1939 | TEXAS A&M, 11–0 | Homer Norton | John Kimbrough, fb | AP, WS, Helms, IFA, TFT |
| | USC, 8–0–2 | Howard Jones | Grenny Lansdell, hb | DS |
| | CORNELL, 8–0 | Carl Snavely | Nick Drahos, t | LS |
| 1938 | TENNESSEE, 11–0 | Bob Neyland | George Cafego, hb | Dunkel, LS, IFA, TFT |
| | TCU, 11–0 | Dutch Meyer | Davey O'Brien, qb | AP, WS, Helms |
| | NOTRE DAME, 8–1 | Elmer Layden | Ed Beinor, t | DS |
| 1937 | PITTSBURGH, 9–0–1 | Jock Sutherland | Marshall Goldberg, hb | AP, DS, LS, IFA, WS, TFT |
| | CALIFORNIA, 10–0–1 | Stub Allison | Vic Bottari, hb | Dunkel, Helms |
| 1936 | MINNESOTA, 7–1 | Bernie Bierman | Andy Uram, hb | AP, Dunkel, LS, DS, Helms |
| | PITTSBURGH, 8–1–1 | Jock Sutherland | Marshall Goldberg, hb | IFA, TFT |
| | LSU, 9–1–1 | Bernie Moore | Gaynell Tinsley, e | WS |
| 1935 | MINNESOTA, 8–0 | Bernie Bierman | Julie Alphonse, qb | LS, IFA, Helms, Davis |
| | SMU, 12–1 | Matty Bell | Bobby Wilson, hb | DS, TFT |
| | PRINCETON, 9–0 | Fritz Crisler | Pepper Constable, fb | Davis (tie), Dunkel |
| | LSU, 9–2 | Bernie Moore | Abe Mickel, qb | WS |

| Year | Team & Record | Coach | Top Player | Selector |
|---|---|---|---|---|
| 1934 | MINNESOTA, 8–0 | Bernie Bierman | Pug Lund, hb | DS, LS, IFA, Helms, Davis |
| | ALABAMA, 10–0 | Frank Thomas | Don Hutson, e | Dunkel, WS, TFT |
| | PITTSBURGH, 8–1 | Jock Sutherland | Izzy Weinstock, fb | Davis (tie) |
| 1933 | MICHIGAN, 7–0–1 | Harry Kipke | Frank Wistert, t | DS, Helms, TFT, IFA, Davis |
| | USC, 10–1–1 | Howard Jones | Cotton Warburton, hb | WS |
| | OHIO STATE, 7–1 | Sam Willaman | Dick Heekins, hb | Dunkel |
| | PRINCETON, 9–0 | Fritz Crisler | Kat Kadlic, qb | Davis (tie) |
| 1932 | USC, 10–0 | Howard Jones | Orv Mohler, hb | IFA, Dunkel, TFT, HF, WS, Davis |
| | MICHIGAN, 8–0 | Harry Kipke | Harry Newman, qb | DS, Davis (tie) |
| | COLGATE, 8–0 | Andy Kerr | Charley Soleau, qb | Davis (tie) |
| 1931 | USC, 10–1 | Howard Jones | Ernie Pinckert, hb | All but Davis |
| | PURDUE, 9–1 | Noble Kizer | Charley Miller, e | Davis |
| | PITTSBURGH, 8–1 | Jock Sutherland | Warren Heller, qb | Davis (tie) |
| 1930 | NOTRE DAME, 10–0 | Knute Rockne | Marchy Schwartz, hb | Unanimous |
| | ALABAMA, 10–0 | Wallace Wade | Fred Sington, t | Davis (tie) |
| 1929 | NOTRE DAME, 9–0 | Knute Rockne | Frank Carideo, qb | DS, Dunkel, IFA, Helms |
| | PITTSBURGH, 9–1 | Jock Sutherland | Joe Donchess, e | Davis |
| | USC, 10–2 | Howard Jones | Russ Saunders, hb | TFT |
| 1928 | GEORGIA TECH, 10–0 | Bill Alexander | Warner Mizell, hb | IFA, Helms, TFT, Davis |
| | USC, 9–0–1 | Howard Jones | Lloyd Thomas, hb | DS |
| | DETROIT, 9–0 | Gus Dorais | Lloyd Brazil, hb | Davis (tie) |
| 1927 | ILLINOIS, 7–0–1 | Bob Zuppke | Russ Crane, c | DS, Davis, Helms |
| | YALE, 7–1 | T. A. D. Jones | Bruce Caldwell, fb | IFA |
| | NOTRE DAME, 7–1–1 | Knute Rockne | Christy Flanagan, hb | TFT |

| Year | Team & Record | Coach | Top Player | Selector |
|---|---|---|---|---|
| 1926 | STANFORD, 10-0-1 | Pop Warner | Ted Shipkey, e | DS |
| | NAVY, 9-0-1 | Bill Ingram | Tom Hamilton, hb | IFA |
| | ALABAMA, 9-0-1 | Wallace Wade | Hoyt Winslett, e | Helms |
| | LAFAYETTE, 9-0 | Herb McCracken | Mike Wilson, hb | Davis |
| 1925 | ALABAMA, 10-0 | Wallace Wade | Johnny Mack Brown, hb | Helms, IFA |
| | DARTMOUTH, 8-0 | Jesse Hawley | Andy Oberlander, hb | DS, Davis |
| 1924 | NOTRE DAME, 10-0 | Knute Rockne | "The Four Horsemen" | DS, Helms, IFA |
| | PENNSYLVANIA, 9-1-1 | Lou Young | Ed McGinley, t | Davis |
| 1923 | ILLINOIS, 8-0 | Bob Zuppke | Red Grange, hb | Unanimous |
| 1922 | CORNELL, 8-0 | Gil Dobie | George Pfann, qb | Unanimous |
| | PRINCETON, 8-0 | Bill Roper | Herb Treat, t | Davis (tie) |
| 1921 | CORNELL, 8-0 | Gil Dobie | Eddie Kaw, hb | Unanimous |
| | IOWA, 7-0 | Howard Jones | Aubrey Devine, hb | Davis (tie) |
| | LAFAYETTE, 9-0 | Jock Sutherland | Frank Schwab, t | Davis (tie) |
| 1920 | CALIFORNIA, 9-0 | Andy Smith | Brick Muller, e | Helms |
| | NOTRE DAME, 9-0 | Knute Rockne | George Gipp, fb | Davis |
| | PRINCETON, 6-0-1 | Bill Roper | Stan Keck, t | Davis (tie) |
| 1919 | HARVARD, 9-0-1 | Bob Fisher | Ed Casey, hb | Unanimous |
| | NOTRE DAME, 9-0 | Knute Rockne | George Gipp, fb | Davis |
| | ILLINOIS, 6-1 | Bob Zuppke | Charley Carney, e | Davis (tie) |
| 1918 | PITTSBURGH, 4-1 | Pop Warner | Tom Davies, hb | Unanimous |
| 1917 | GEORGIA TECH, 9-0 | John Heisman | George Strupper, hb | Unanimous |
| 1916 | PITTSBURGH, 8-0 | Pop Warner | Bob Peck, c | Unanimous |
| | ARMY, 9-0 | Charley Daly | John McEwan, c | Davis (tie) |

| Year | Team & Record | Coach | Top Player | Selector |
|---|---|---|---|---|
| 1915 | CORNELL, 9–0 | Al Sharpe | Charley Barrett, hb | Unanimous |
|  | PITTSBURGH, 8–0 | Pop Warner | Bob Peck, c | Davis (tie) |
| 1914 | ARMY, 9–0 | Charley Daly | John McEwan, c | Unanimous |
|  | ILLINOIS, 7–0 | Bob Zuppke | Perry Graves, e | Davis (tie) |
| 1913 | HARVARD, 9–0 | Percy Haughton | Eddie Mahan, fb | Unanimous |
|  | CHICAGO, 7–0 | Amos Alonzo Stagg | Paul Des Jardien, c | Davis (tie) |
| 1912 | HARVARD, 9–0 | Percy Haughton | Charley Brickley, hb | Unanimous |
| 1911 | PRINCETON, 8–0–2 | Bill Roper | Sanford White, e | Unanimous |
| 1910 | HARVARD, 8–0–1 | Percy Haughton | Percy Wendell, hb | Unanimous |
| 1909 | YALE, 10–0 | Howard Jones | Ted Coy, fb | Unanimous |
| 1908 | PENNSYLVANIA, 11–0–1 | Sol Metzger | Hunter Scarlett, e | Unanimous |
| 1907 | YALE, 9–0–1 | Bill Knox | T. A. D. Jones, hb | Unanimous |
| 1906 | PRINCETON, 9–0–1 | Bill Roper | Ed Dillon, hb | Helms |
|  | YALE, 9–0–1 | Foster Rockwell | Hugh Knox, hb | Davis |
| 1905 | CHICAGO, 11–0 | Amos Alonzo Stagg | Walter Eckersall, qb | Helms |
|  | YALE, 10–0 | Jack Owsley | Tom Shevlin, e | Davis |
| 1904 | PENNSYLVANIA, 12–0 | Carl Williams | Andy Smith, hb | Unanimous |
| 1903 | PRINCETON, 11–0 | Art Hillebrand | John DeWitt, g | Unanimous |
| 1902 | MICHIGAN, 11–0 | Fielding H. Yost | Willie Heston, hb | Unanimous |
|  | YALE, 11–0–1 | Joe Swan | Tom Shevlin, e | Davis (tie) |
| 1901 | MICHIGAN, 11–0 | Fielding H. Yost | Willie Heston, hb | Helms |
|  | HARVARD, 12–0 | Bill Reid | Robert Kernan, hb | Davis |
| 1900 | YALE, 12–0 | Malcolm McBride | Perry Hale, hb | Unanimous |

| Year | Team & Record | Coach | Top Player | Selector |
| --- | --- | --- | --- | --- |
| 1899 | HARVARD, 10–0–1 | Ben Dibblee | Charley Daly, qb | Helms |
|  | PRINCETON, 12–1 | No Coach | Arthur Poe, e | Davis |
| 1898 | HARVARD, 11–0 | Cameron Forbes | Charley Daly, qb | Helms |
|  | PRINCETON, 11–0–1 | No Coach | Lew Palmer, e | Davis |
| 1897 | PENNSYLVANIA, 15–0 | George Woodruff | T. Truxton Hare, g | Unanimous |
|  | YALE, 9–0–2 | Frank Butterworth | Charles DeSaulles, hb | Davis (tie) |
| 1896 | PRINCETON, 10–0–1 | No Coach | Addison Kelly, hb | Unanimous |
|  | LAFAYETTE, 11–0–1 | S. B. Newton | Fielding H. Yost, t | Davis (tie) |
| 1895 | PENNSYLVANIA, 14–0 | George Woodruff | Charles Gelbert, e | Unanimous |
|  | YALE, 13–0–2 | John Hartwell | Samuel Thorne, hb | Davis (tie) |
| 1894 | YALE, 16–0 | Bill Rhodes | William Hickok, g | Unanimous |
|  | PENNSYLVANIA, 12–0 | George Woodruff | George Brooke, e | Davis (tie) |
| 1893 | PRINCETON, 11–0 | No Coach | Philip King, hb | Helms |
|  | YALE, 10–1 | Bill Rhodes | Frank Butterworth, fb | Davis |
| 1892 | YALE, 13–0 | Walter Camp | Frank Hinkey, e | Unanimous |
| 1891 | YALE, 13–0 | Walter Camp | Pudge Heffelfinger, e | Unanimous |
| 1890 | HARVARD, 11–0 | George Stewart | Marshall Newell, t | Unanimous |
| 1889 | PRINCETON, 10–0 | No Coach | Edgar Allan Poe, hb | Unanimous |